T0160045

A Snowflake's Guide to Christmas

How to survive a deeply problematic holiday

Also by Dave Skinner

Why Steve Was Late

A Snowflake's Guide to Christmas

How to survive a deeply problematic holiday

DAVE SKINNER

Atlantic Books
London

Published in hardback in Great Britain in 2020 by Atlantic Books,
an imprint of Atlantic Books Ltd.

10 9 8 7 6 5 4 3 2 1

Illustrations by Carmen R. Balit unless otherwise noted

A CIP catalogue record for this book is available from the British Library.

Hardback ISBN: 978 1 83895 209 9
E-book ISBN: 978 1 83895 210 5

Printed in Great Britain

Atlantic Books
An imprint of Atlantic Books Ltd
Ormond House
26–27 Boswell Street
London
WC1N 3JZ

www.atlantic-books.co.uk

To Sal, Charlie, Grace and
all the Snowflakes everywhere

Contents

Christmas is a time for snowflakes...

Introduction

Like so many things that predate Instagram, Christmas can be a deeply problematic season for any compassionate, contemporary person who considers themselves switched-on, sensitive and socially engaged. Outwardly a time of light-hearted fun and celebration, it's arguably a motorway pile-up of intersectional issues.

But also for Snowflakes...

When else are you likely to find so many people of different generations, often with such diverse beliefs and opinions, compelled to come together? Usually in a confined, overly warm, heavily tinselled domestic environment, where there are astonishing amounts of free alcohol on tap, where old grievances and familial recriminations can quickly bubble over, and where there is a constant underlying pressure to HAVE FUN.

Aside from all the potentially explosive 'chat', Christmas is a time of colossal consumption. Not just of vast quantities of booze and food (especially heartbreaking, climate crisis-inducing meat), but also of STUFF.

Christmas is all about exchanging stuff: plastic stuff, shiny stuff, sparkly stuff – much of which cannot be recycled. You're obliged, by the unspoken laws of the festive season, to give people stuff you're not entirely sure they'll want – and, in return, to receive and say 'thank you' for stuff you don't really want or need.

Frankly, for a modern millennial, Yuletide can be a merry freaking minefield.

This book is here to help.

Whether you yourself are a loud, proud, wide a-woke Snowflake, you're related to one, or you work with one – and need to give him/her/they/them a 'Secret Santa' gift – this invaluable guide is packed full of relevant and contemporary festive hacks, hints and tips designed to help you navigate this most troubling of holidays.

Over the following pages, *A Snowflake's Guide to Christmas* breaks down the component parts of the 'classic Christmas', identifies where the most problematic triggers lie, then offers advice and solutions to help achieve safe passage through the potentially choppy Christmas waters...

A note on terminology

The current use of the word 'Snowflake' as a derogatory term for liberal-minded, easily offended individuals has its origins in Chuck Palahniuk's 1996 novel *Fight Club*, in which a member of the anarchist group Project Mayhem tells the other members, 'You are not a beautiful and unique snowflake.'

Recent events (Brexit, Trump, the climate emergency, the verbal diarrhoea of Katie Hopkins) have brought the term into widespread use, particularly in the right-wing press, where it is used to lambast anyone with even the vaguest hint of a conscience.

For many people, even the word 'Snowflake' itself has a triggering effect, and some may question its use in this book (I call these people 'meta-Snowflakes').

The author uses the term here in an attempt to 'reappropriate' it, throwing it back in the faces of those who use it to stigmatize us. So be loud, proud progressives and reclaim the label, and remember... enough Snowflakes can make an avalanche.

The 'Are you a Snowflake?' checklist

Before you begin reading this book, you may want to check whether you are, in fact, a Snowflake.

Take a look at these questions, which should help you decide how strong your Snowflake status may or may not be:

1. Is this girl...?

a) A heroine, one of the most important voices in the modern world

b) A bit intense

c) Annoying

2. Is this man...?

a) A force for evil, one of the most hateful figures in the modern world

b) Probably just as bad as all the other politicians

c) Doing a great job!

3. When you see this, do you want to...?

a) Scream, shout and sob at the sheer inhumanity of it all

b) Give Veganuary a try

c) Get a milkshake

4. If someone gave you this, would you...?

a) Glue yourself to the nearest train, as a mark of protest against climate change

b) Put it in a drawer with the spare batteries, keys, screws and rubber bands, and forget about it

c) Use it to assemble the scale model you're building of the world's biggest passenger airliner – the massive (and gorgeous) Airbus A380.

5. When you look into one of these, do you see...?

a) A unique and precious individual, capable of extraordinary things and deserving of every opportunity to be the best version of themselves

b) Someone who could probably make a bit more of an effort

c) Muggins

If you answered all or **mostly A**s, congratulations, you are a bona fide, card-carrying Snowflake.

If you answered **mostly C**s, you are not at all a Snowflake – in fact, you are a 'Noflake'.

If you plumped for **mostly B**s, you sit roughly midway on the spectrum of Snowflakery. By the end of this book, you might well find you've gone further one way or the other...

The good news is, whatever result you came up with, this guide has something to offer *everyone* as Christmas approaches. So, without further ado, let's crack on.

The Problem with Christmas Trees

You don't need to be Greta T to know that trees are beautiful, precious, life-giving... Now more than ever we should celebrate and cherish them; they are the carbon-cleansing lungs of this poor, beleaguered planet.

So, let's be honest, there's something more than a little problematic about growing a Christmas tree, only to chop it down in the prime of its life, stick it in the corner of a living room, festoon it with cheap tinsel and fairy lights, then watch it slowly die. You wouldn't do it to a cow, so why do it to a conifer?

Like the turkey – another of the great losers in the Yuletide game – Christmas trees have long been the woody victims of systemic oppression.

Denied their true names in the cause of consumerism, the noble Douglas fir, majestic Fraser fir, fragrant balsam fir and countless proud pines are rebranded as generic, anonymous 'Christmas trees'. Intensively farmed all year round, saplings are cultivated with limited space and in vast numbers – like green, branchy, battery hens. Then they are

Jack @Jack99Croydon

Happy NY. Unless you're a Christmas tree... They're lying in the street up and down my road, like dead prostitutes... Makes me want to cry all day. #friendofthefir literally cut off in their prime and displaced from the other so-called 'Christmas trees', squirrels and associated woodland creatures they've come to know – only to be pimped with gaudy decorations and heavy baubles, then unceremoniously chucked outside into the cold by 5th January.

It's an ecological horror story.

From this...

To this...

And then this.

9

Possible Solutions

❄ Rather than cut a tree down and kill it, you could give it a little holiday in your home... Increasingly, garden centres and nurseries offer a **Christmas-tree hire service**. Often, they'll even deliver and collect the tree to save you the bother. It's a win-win: you get to have a tree for the festive season, the tree gets a change of scene – and, best of all, it can carry on growing after it's returned. (Just make sure it's grown sustainably, by looking for the FSC or Soil Association logo.)

❄ Instead of a Christmas 'tree', why not welcome a **Christmas pot plant** into your home? An aloe vera plant requires very little care, costs less than £10, and will live for years, given a little TLC. A nice silk ribbon around its pot will make it 'pop' for Christmas and saves the environmental cost and headache of stringy, tangled lights. As a bonus, the leaves contain a clear gel that can help heal first- and second-degree burns. So, if your neighbour's twinkly illuminations set their conventional Christmas tree on fire and burn their house down, you can offer more than just a cup of cocoa...

❄ **Draw or paint a picture of a Christmas tree.** All this requires is a large piece of paper, a little artistic imagination and a few blobs of Blu-Tack. Alternatively, coat a wall with blackboard paint (available in all good DIY stores) and draw a jolly Christmas tree using coloured chalk. Friends and family can muck in, and you can change the tree and its decorations every day if you like... Christmas cactus? Christmas oak? Christmas monkey puzzle tree? Anything's possible...

If a friend or family member (probably of a different generation) takes issue with these Christmas tree alternatives, why not suggest that they become a **human Christmas tree**. Offer to drape them in tinsel and lights, and hang baubles from any piercings they might have. Make a space in the corner amongst the presents, where they can stand still and silent, largely ignored, with their arms outstretched for a few hours.

#SolidarityWithThePine #ScrewYouAuntieSue

The Problem with Christmas Crackers

Interesting historical fact: Christmas crackers were first devised around 1845–1850 by a London sweet-maker called Tom Smith.

On a trip to Paris, Tom had seen the French 'bonbon' sweets (almonds wrapped in pretty paper) and had tried, fairly unsuccessfully, to sell these back home, accompanied by a small motto or riddle. Legend has it that Tom was sitting in front of a crackling, popping log fire, when inspiration hit him… Wouldn't it be fun if his sweets, or even toys, could be accompanied by a 'crack' when their elaborate wrappers were pulled in half!

After much R&D, in 1861 Tom launched what he called his 'Bangs of Expectation', and the rest is history…

For today's ecologically aware, environmentally sensitive soul, the principal problem with Christmas crackers is that they are to 'low waste' what RuPaul is to 'shy and retiring'. (A secondary problem is that they are, by and large, crap.)

A typical Christmas family braced for cracker-based disappointment

Modern-day crackers are, generally, over-priced and underwhelming. The bang you get – if you get one at all – rarely lives up to the buck that was spent. Worse than the waste of money and the post-pull anticlimax, though, is the cracker's anti-eco status: shiny, foil-coated or glittery cardboard crackers cannot be recycled.

To add insult to injury – like swearing at Mother Nature and then kicking her in the shins – they usually contain a 'surprise' you don't want or need, often made out of non-recyclable, single-use plastic. All that, and you get a scrap of paper with a joke that's staler than last year's Christmas stuffing – whether you want it or not.

Just a few of the Christmas cracker 'surprises' you don't need or want, and which cannot be 'unmade'... 'Game of microscopic skittles, anyone?'

It's time the cracker was called out as the pointless, wasteful, eco hand grenade it really is.

Five Things You're Unlikely To Hear After The Pulling Of A Christmas Cracker

1. ❄ 'OMG! A plastic jumping frog! I LOVE it!'

2. ❄ 'This flimsy paper crown makes me feel like the actual Queen of England!'

3. ❄ 'Yikes, that bang was so spectacular I think Grandad might be having a heart attack!'

4. ❄ 'This tiny, ineffectual plastic magnifying glass will be invaluable to me in my work as a hairdresser. I will treasure it ALWAYS.'

5. ❄ 'There's real wisdom in this "truth-telling fish". From now on, for every major life decision – I'm going to consult it first!'

Possible Solutions

If you think the absence of crackers at your Christmas table will lead to a festive family uprising – tears, anger, possibly even violence – there are companies online that make more sustainable, 'bespoke' or 'curated' crackers. However, these tend to be expensive, and most people born after 1995 need to save their precious pennies to pay for rent, clothes and electric Ubers.

Why not save your money and the planet's resources, by sharing 'virtual crackers' with your loved ones? Not only are these cheap, they're fun and can be tailored to the person you 'pull' them with...

⚠ How To Pull A Virtual Cracker

1. Turn to the person immediately next to you, gently hold their wrists up in front of their face about six inches apart, then swiftly clap their hands together. At the point of impact shout, 'Bang!' or 'Crack!', or, if you'd prefer, something else – for example: 'Wow!', 'Howzat!', or 'Shit the bed!'.

2. In place of a traditional paper 'crown', put on their head one of your own hats from your personal collection: a woolly hat you knitted yourself, a nice beanie, a beret, a fedora, a fez, whatever you've got. (Don't forget to get your hat back at the end of proceedings. Beanies, berets, fedoras and fezzes don't grow on trees and will last a lifetime if you take care of them.)

3. Swap out a small, useless, disposable plastic 'gift', for something larger, more meaningful and longer lasting – the gift of wisdom. Look the person next to you in the eye and tell them 'a truth', for example:

'Life is like riding a bicycle. To keep your balance, you must keep moving.' – Albert Einstein

'The world will see you the way you see you, and treat you the way you treat yourself.' – Beyoncé

'Uncle Ian, that moustache makes you look like a paedophile.'

4. Instead of reading them a corny joke with a clunky Christmas pun, find a different way to make them laugh – for example: tickle them/randomly blow a loud, wet raspberry at the youngest, oldest or most pompous person seated at the table/make an extravagant and surprising claim, e.g. 'This Christmas, I've shaved the cat!'

5. Hug them briefly but firmly, then move on.

Alternative Christmas Cracker Jokes

Knock, knock
Who's there?
Cow says
Cow says who?
No, a cow says, 'Moo.' And then it says, 'Why do you continue to persecute me like this? You can get milk from ice, almonds, even coconuts – you heartless monster!'

Who's a Snowflake's favourite festive pop star?
Beyon-sleigh!

Why would Santa Claus never make demands on the already overstretched NHS?
Because he has private elf care.

How do you know Santa came down your chimney?
Because the carpet's covered in his carbon footprints.

Why did the little polar bear cry?
Because he had his gloves and scarf, but he'd lost his ice cap.

Why did the turkey cross the road?
To get into an Uber and get the hell out of town.

What's Donald Trump's favourite Christmas confectionery?
A Chocolate Orange.

The Problem with Carol Singers

In what world would anyone think it was okay to gather together a gang, knock on a stranger's door, sing a medley of quasi-religious and outmoded songs at them, then demand money to go away again? It's like a flash mob crossed with a mugging, an orchestrated act of audio-aggression, a deliberate infringement of a person's basic space and rights, all dressed up as festive fun.

Welcome to Christmas carolling.

Bad...

Worse...

The dictionary describes a carol as *'a joyful hymn or religious song, especially one celebrating the birth of Christ'*, so tough luck if you happen to follow a different religious path, or you're not interested in/are sceptical about the true story of baby J.

Unfortunately, most carollers don't take this into account: their motto is *'You get what you get, and you don't get upset.'* If they do take requests, chances are it'll be a golden oldie – they'll be unlikely to belt out anything by Beyoncé, David Guetta or Lizzo.

So, if confronted by carollers, what should you do...?

Possible Solutions

❄ **A large water pistol.** Greta T and the Extinction Rebellion protesters have demonstrated that actions speak louder than words, that disrupting normal practices can spark debate and ultimately effect change. The 'Super Soaker Hydra' is available online (priced at approx. £15), and will swiftly dampen the spirits and mock Victorian garb of even a sizeable group of earnest Yuletide yodellers. If this seems too extreme, you could replace the water with a festive-themed liquid – for example, lukewarm mulled wine might soften the blow.

❄ **A sign on the front door** which reads: *'I am deaf, please don't try to sing at me. In doing so, you merely highlight the difference between myself and those who are able-eared. Please save us both the embarrassment – and you the strain to your vocal cords – and move on. Merry Christmas.'*

❄ **Fight fire with (musical) fire.** Open the door, smile encouragingly and listen politely as the singers progress through their Judeo-Christian/Santa-themed set list. Then, when they've finished and ask you for a small donation, say 'My turn!' and sing back at them. Sing something you enjoy – Taylor Swift's 'Shake It Off', Sia's 'Chandelier', maybe something by Korean boy-band sensation BTS... Just really give it some welly, then bid them a festive farewell and shut the door.

The Problem with Christmas Shopping

According to the Bible, the original Christmas gift-givers were three kings, who – being royalty – could stretch to gold, frankincense and myrrh. Hopefully, they selected these must-have items from their local, independently run gold, frankincense and myrrh outlets, and did their bit to 'shop local'. **#SaveTheHighStreet**

(Don't worry, no one knows what myrrh is – or frankincense for that matter. According to Wikipedia, myrrh is a kind of natural gum or resin – obtained from a small, thorny tree – that has been used throughout history as a perfume. And frankincense is an aromatic gum obtained from a different tree, also used as a perfume. So they're both pretty similar. Either way, spin forward 2,000+ years, and they're the kind of thing Gwyneth Paltrow would be selling online for $500 a pot.)

These days, instead of trekking miles across deserts via camel and starlight, they'd have just gone online, made a few clicks and had Amazon Prime courier their pressies to Bethlehem that same day – via a delivery driver on a donkey with built-in satnav.

There was a time when Christmas gifts were hand-made: carved wooden toys... knitted teddy bears... patchwork quilts... an orange studded with cloves to keep your Victorian undergarments smelling nice... simple stuff, crafted with care and given with love.

Nowadays, thanks to mass merchandising, mass marketing and mass manufacturing, Christmas gift-giving can present a mass of potential problems...

Beware Black Friday!

Like the music of Ed Sheeran, Black Friday has grown in strength and spread its influence around the world – and now consumers across the planet are held, helpless, in its spell. Deep down, we suspect we should just ignore it, even turn away from it, *but we can't.* **#TooDamnCatchy**

Black Friday, Oxford Circus, 2019

Interesting historical fact:

'Black Friday' is believed to have originated in Philadelphia in the early 1960s. It was a name used to describe the inevitable snarl-up of traffic and people that would happen on the Friday after Thanksgiving, as eager shoppers went Christmas crackers.

In the run-up to 'BF', brands bombard us with adverts for amazing savings and once-in-a-lifetime offers. Gripped by FOMO, people will queue around the block, fight, even *kill* one another to bag a bargain: apparently, since 2006, there have been 12 reported deaths in the US and 117 Black Friday-associated injuries.

What's remarkable about many of the objects fought over on Black Friday is that people subsequently realize they never really wanted or needed them. It seems that, in the heat of the moment, a kind of discount-driven frenzy comes over them – a 'black mist' descends...

Across the world, on the day after Black Friday (which retailers secretly refer to as 'Sanity Saturday'), dazed, scratched and bruised shoppers wake up – like Bruce Banner in his torn and bloodied post-Hulk clothes – and look in shock and confusion at the scene around them. '*Why,*' they think, '*did I buy that cut-price cappuccino-making machine? I don't even like coffee... Can I really have wanted that heavily discounted cat tree scratching post with fun platforms, caves and ramps? I don't have a cat... What was I THINKING when I punched that old woman, so that I could take home the bargain basement inflatable hot tub with in-built Prosecco pump? Prosecco makes me gassy.*'

Perhaps the smartest thing any self-respecting, socially conscious individual can do on Black Friday is go for a long walk – ideally in nature – as far away as possible from any major retailers. Failing that, spend the day visiting art galleries, museums, the cinema... Or volunteer at an old people's home, hospital or soup kitchen. Whatever you do, stay out of the shops and offline – or you too may fall foul of the siren song of Black Friday.

Remember, Black Friday is evil. As is Cyber Monday. And the thankfully short-lived 'Spunk It Sunday'.

CALL-OUT CORNER
Celebrity Christmas Scents

Celebrity 'scents' are cynical, bottled nonsense. If you really want to smell like Victoria Beckham, Gemma Collins or Phillip Schofield, instead of spending £50+ on a fancy bottle of scented water, why not write to them and ask if they'll give you an old T-shirt/socks/pair of boxer shorts that they were going to throw out. Don't wash whatever they send you and wear with pride – that way you can smell like your fave celeb, save water and do your bit to recycle.

The Problem with Gifts for Children

We need to be brave and open about this: buying Christmas presents for children in modern, Western society is a daunting task that can potentially lead to mental health issues.

In modern Britain, most young people are putting off having kids until their late twenties or early thirties. But just because you don't have sprogs of your own, that doesn't mean you're necessarily in the clear; you may well have friends or relatives with young children, and they will consider you quite the prize-winning A-hole if you don't give their progeny some kind of gift at Christmas.

The problem is that the vast majority of toys are made of hard plastic – or a variety of different plastics – and cannot be recycled as part of your regular household recycling collection. Even more traditional wooden toys can be tricky to dispose of as many of them have been painted, varnished or in some way 'finished' so that they can't be recycled. Pity poor Pinocchio – destined always to be a wooden boy, never to be recycled into a funky table lamp.

Toys that are in good working order can be sold on, donated to a charity shop or a local church, a toy library or a playgroup – so you could salve your conscience by giving a toy at Christmas and encouraging the young recipient to *'play with it for a bit, then pass it on'*. Just try your best to be prepared for whatever reaction this might elicit from a confused/horrified/outraged four-year-old. **#TinyFistsOfFury, #ToddlerTerror, #ImAnUncleGetMeOutOfHere**

If you do decide to take the path of least resistance and buy toys for Christmas presents, no one will blame you. However, you should brace yourself for the blinkered and outmoded gender stereotyping that persists in Toy Land. Even in 2020, this largely remains a world where the status quo maintains that little girls like dressing up dolls and little boys like shooting guns... Where pink, sparkly or rainbow-coloured stuff is for Jane (and her friend Cutie Pie the Dream Unicorn), while camo is for John (and his pal G.I. Joe).

If you don't want to perpetuate these simplistic, binary gender stereotypes, why not play the sexist, outmoded, injection-moulded plastic toy peddlers at their own game, and make your own child-friendly Christmas presents...?

CALL-OUT CORNER
Chocolate Coins

Hello?! In case you hadn't noticed, there is a global diabetes crisis. Giving chocolate coins to children is like giving the contents of a hotel mini-bar to a recovering alcoholic. It's downright irresponsible. As well as rotting their teeth and spiking their blood sugar, those coins are indoctrinating the young into a life of joyless capitalism. Plus, the shiny, metallic wrappers can't be recycled. This Christmas, switch out the chocolate currency for a good, old-fashioned satsuma. Plenty of vitamin C to ward off scurvy and the peel can go in the compost. Two thumbs up!

Three Gender Stereotype-Disrupting Toys You Can Make Yourself

1. ❄ **Personalized Puzzle.** Start with a sheet of cardboard or paper, (which can be recycled further down the line). Draw and take time to enjoy colouring in an image of your choosing – then cut it up into jigsaw-shaped pieces for a child to reassemble. Your drawing could be of something light-hearted, festive and neutral – e.g. a kitten and a puppy high-fiving in front of a log fire. Or you could make a political point – e.g. Greta T wrestling Donald Trump to the floor in a headlock. Or you could use your home-made puzzle to introduce a younger person to a modern role model – e.g. Emma Watson, Todrick Hall or the cast of Queer Eye. Just have fun!

2. ❄ **Potato Person.** Again, this is a great DIY Christmas toy. Inspired by the outdated, unrecyclable, hard plastic Mr. Potato Head, give the child in your life the chance to create their own Mx. Potato Person. Gift them a *real* potato (a large King Edward or Maris Piper would be ideal – perhaps in an old shoebox), along with a variety of 'facial features' made out of other vegetables (e.g. radish disc 'eyes', a baby sweetcorn 'nose', mushroom 'ears'...). The child will have hours of fun, taking their 'blank canvas' potato on a gender-fluid journey. And at the end of that journey – with the help of a responsible adult – they can cook and eat their delicious toy. Nothing wasted, and, potentially, all of the recommended five-a-day in one delicious, vegan-friendly hit.

3. ✳ **Real-Life Robot.** Forget Siri and Alexa – they're burning up the planet's resources and creepily listening in on your life and shopping habits. It's time to go old-school android... Amazon packaging accounts for a huge amount of recycling at Christmas time. So gather up all the cardboard boxes you can scavenge, get your trusty colouring pens and create your own 'robot outfit' that you can wear over your clothes. Present yourself to the child in question, and tell them, 'Hi, I'm your Christmas robot buddy.' Then offer them a period of time (no more than an hour) when you'll do whatever they say (within reason). You don't *have* to, but if you want, you can adopt a funny robot voice. And when playtime's over, together with the child you can break down the costume, tear it up and put it in the recycling. Even if they cry at the time, they'll thank you in the long run for a fun lesson about sustainability!

The Problem with Gifts for Grown-Ups

This is controversial, so check the company you're in before saying it out loud, but... There *is* a school of thought that believes Christmas is really for kids, not for adults. This is especially true when it comes to presents.

Broadly speaking, there are three categories of Christmas presents traded by adults:

1 **Boring/Sensible Gifts:** In this category you might find: socks, underpants, shaving equipment, skincare products, a pen, shower gel, a screwdriver set, a French road atlas, a nice candle. The accepted response upon receiving one of these gifts is:

'Oh! Yes... Thanks... I need a new [insert boring gift here]... Lovely...'

2 **Easy/Lazy Gifts:** We're talking money or a gift voucher. If you and your loved ones agree to exchange actual money, you can dispense with all the usual Christmas present-opening niceties and literally pass a twenty-pound note from person to person. If you're lucky, it might even work its way around the room and come back to you! The accepted response upon receiving a gift voucher is:

'Oh! A voucher, for [insert name of shop here – e.g. M&S/Halfords/Ann Summers]. That's great, thanks!' This is either delivered with genuine warmth and pleasure or through a false smile as you secretly think, *'I **never** shop in M&S/Halfords/Ann Summers, you idiot! I'd rather have had the cash!'*

3 **Wacky/Novelty Gifts:** For any switched-on, environmentally conscious, sympathetic person with a degree of taste, this is where some of the most problematic Yuletide gifts can be found – the ones that are *kind of* funny for a moment, yes, but that probably won't be cherished and passed from generation to generation. The following are all real gifts available to buy this Christmas, none of which is likely to achieve 'future heirloom' status:

- A big box of nothing (literally, an empty cardboard box – £8)

- Novelty candles (including the scents of 'sweaty balls' and 'fanny farts' – £5)

- A poo in a box (a realistic-looking plastic poo in a gift box – £6.50)

- The Father Christmas face toilet seat cover (£8.99)

- A pair of socks with the word 'TWAT' embroidered on them (£5.99)

Alternative Christmas Jumpers

Rather than flocking to the usual high-street retailers, try knitting a Christmas jumper for a loved one. For extra Snowflake points, use one of these progressive designs:

Interestingly, in the Grown-Ups' Christmas Gift Venn Diagram (below) you can see there is actually quite a lot of overlap between Boring/Sensible Gifts and Wacky/Novelty Gifts.

For more on SECRET SANTA GIFTS – see 'The Problem with Office Christmas Parties', page 77.

Increasingly, forward-thinking, sustainability-sensitive people are less interested in physical objects and possessions, and more interested in 'experiences'. If you'd like to give the grown-ups in your life gifts, but would rather not conform to the usual Yuletide stereotypes, here are some ideas for alternative Christmas presents that won't cost the earth – financially or environmentally – but could make for happy memories:

1. ❆ **An I.O.U.** Instead of giving someone a voucher or gift, explain that this Christmas you've used the money you would have spent on them on somebody else who's not so well off. Homeless shelters are especially grateful for donations of clothing during the cold winter months. Or you could donate to a food bank – you can buy a lot of tinned food for the price of a plastic poo in a box... Take a snap of what you did with the money to show to your friend or family member – any short-term pangs of disappointment should quickly give way to a festive, feel-good glow inside.

2. ❆ **A passport to dog-borrowing fun.** For under £20 a year, you can subscribe to a dog-borrowing website (e.g. www.borrowmydoggy.com) that connects dog owners with dog lovers who don't necessarily have the space, time or money to take on a dog of their own – but would be happy to help with the odd walk now and then. It's true, a dog is for life, not just for Christmas – but this way, a dog can be for Christmas, and not for life.

3. ❆ **A big bag of leaves.** Everyone enjoys strolling through woods, kicking leaves. So, from autumn onwards, keep your eyes peeled, collect the leaves you see on the ground and dry them out. Then, come 25th December, present your loved one with a big (biodegradable) bag of crisp, colourful leaves. They can tip these out on the carpet and together you can take a stroll, arm in arm, around the living room – imagining you're out and about in the bracing cold. Afterwards, gather the leaves up and put them on the compost, or leave them in a hedgehog-friendly heap in the corner of the garden.

4. ❆ **A lovely warm bath.** Television execs are perpetually trying to come up with programme ideas that are like 'a lovely warm bath'. What could be more like a lovely warm bath than an actual lovely warm bath? In place of a pair of 'TWAT' socks, offer to run your loved one's bath for them. And if you really love them, maybe share the bath, to make the water go further...

CALL-OUT CORNER
Gift Wrapping

If you do decide to give someone a physical gift – ideally something you've crafted yourself, baked or upcycled – do not wrap it. Or at least, don't wrap it in conventional Christmas wrapping paper. Shiny and festive as it is, much of it can't be recycled. Instead, why not use one of the following:

❋ **Plain brown paper:** To check if wrapping paper can be recycled or not, do the 'scrunch test'. Scrunch up the paper in your hand, then let it go. If the paper stays scrunched up, then it can be recycled. If it starts to unfold by itself, it's likely to contain non-recyclable elements. You can also use the 'scrunch test' to check whether or not an egg has been hard-boiled, but it's not recommended...

❋ **Leftover newspaper**: If using newspaper, just be mindful of that day's headlines... No one wants to have to explain *'Pervert Prison Paedos To Get The Vote!'* to a bemused six-year-old.

❋ **Fabric:** A scarf can also double as a present, but don't feel you need to stop there. All manner of clothes can double as wrapping. You could give new underpants wrapped up in old underpants. (Just make sure they're clean.)

The Problem with Christmas Decorations

'Deck the halls with boughs of holly... Fa la la la la la la la la!' goes the traditional, nonsensical Christmas carol. But, for all that it sounds like the kind of thing a mad person might shout as they ran, naked, through the Yuletide streets, there's a really sane, sustainable message in those lyrics.

Instead of decking your halls (living room) with sparkly Christmas decorations and shiny tinsel that can't be recycled, why not go back to nature and *embrace the holly!* (Not literally.)

Rather than buy a plastic wreath or fake festive foliage manufactured in China, you could have a fun afternoon with family and friends, foraging in the great outdoors for the component parts of your own home-grown, home-made decorations.

Gather together a few lichen-dusted twigs and branches, sprigs of holly, ivy, mistletoe, laurel or yew, along with a handful of aesthetically pleasing pine cones, and with a little artistic effort you can create something really lovely and totally natural – an organic addition to your home that would make Frodo Baggins, Maleficent or Kirstie Allsopp proud.

Christmas Lights

Self-expression is a fundamental human right. People should be allowed to express themselves – especially when it comes to *visual* expression, through art, sculpture and display... It's important to remember that the number of Christmas lights your family, friends or neighbours decide to put in their windows and outside their homes is, ultimately, *their* choice. For some people, just a few discreet lights are enough. But for others, the blinking, twinkling, sparkling ribbons of electrified illumination are like crack cocaine.

If someone close to you insists on blinging up their home with lights, you could helpfully let them know that if every UK household swapped a string of incandescent lights for its LED equivalent, we could save over 29,000 tonnes of CO_2, just over the twelve days of Christmas. You could tell them that LEDs are much more environmentally friendly than traditional, twinkling incandescent lights, because they use up to 80% less energy. You could also encourage them to switch to solar-powered lights outdoors, and to put both sets of lights on a timer – that way, they'll not only make environmental savings but save money on their energy bill too.

If all of that falls on deaf ears – because they're too busy admiring the 30-foot high, 400,000 megawatt, illuminated, mechanical, waving Santa they've just erected in their front garden – why not treat yourself to a new pair of bamboo-framed sunglasses for Christmas.

Have fun, but be careful: the leaves and berries of these plants are poisonous (some fatal!) if consumed, so don't bring them into the house if you have pets or children. #XmasHamsterHorror

This...

...is a gateway drug to this...

If you'd rather stay inside in the warm, you could head to the kitchen and make *edible* Christmas decorations – for yourself, or to give as gifts. Gingerbread men – and *women* (#GenderNeutralGingerbread) – can be strung together to make delicious bunting... Instead of glass or plastic baubles you could use iced biscuits shaped like stars, angels, Christmas trees... Switch out unrecyclable tinsel for an irresistible threaded popcorn-and-marshmallow version... Search 'edible Christmas decorations' online for heaps of great ideas. Just try not to eat them all before 25th December!

But do try to eat them *fairly* close to that date. These aren't the kind of decorations you should pack away and stick in the loft until next year...

The Problem
with Christmas Cards

Once upon a time – back when people thought smoking was cool and *good for you* – getting your Christmas card game together was a big deal: you needed to keep on top of the list of loved ones, know their postal addresses, get hold of appropriately festive cards (obvs), buy stamps (ditto), and find time in your life to actually sit down and write something meaningful to all these people (many of whom, in truth, you hadn't had any other contact with all year long).

Then you had to remember to get the cards themselves in the post – factoring in the great Christmas card postal frenzy and subsequent strikes/delays – so that they were delivered before 25th December. Sending someone a Christmas card late, although forgivable, is effectively a way of saying, '*I love you – but not enough to get this to you on time. You're great, but you are, ultimately, an afterthought.*'

Once, people would actually joke, '*Well, that's Debbie crossed off my Christmas card list! If she can't remember to feed my cat while I'm away, she won't be getting a card from ME!*' To be crossed off a person's Christmas card list was to be cast out, sent into the wilderness and eventually forgotten – like Zayn Malik leaving One Direction.

These days, it's estimated that a quarter of people in the UK no longer bother sending old-fashioned, physical Christmas cards. Either there's an army of Grinches out there, gleefully ignoring festive traditions (and presumably sniggering to themselves as they steal Christmas candy from babies, and troll tweeting Yuletide revellers), or Christmas cards have gone high-tech.

The e-card is increasingly popular: digital 'cards' don't cost anything, they're quick, and they can do all sorts of entertaining, animated stuff that an 'analogue' card can't do. Undoubtedly, it's fun to 'open' an e-Christmas card and see an animated snowball do a little dance while singing '*Merry Christmas to you, you smell like a poo!*' before launching itself into the face of Donald Trump – but where's the romance? Where's the sense of time taken and thought given?

Christmas cards present the contemporary citizen with an interconnected web of difficulties, problems and conflicting tensions – which can be broadly summed up in the diagram opposite...

The Christmas Card Conundrum

CHRISTMAS CARD

GOOD (kind, thoughtful, festive)

— vs —

BAD (wasteful, unrecyclable, expensive)

e-CHRISTMAS CARD

GOOD (funny, sustainable, easy)

— vs —

BAD (cold, soulless, too easy, potentially harmful to the career prospects/income of hard-working, dog-harassed postal workers)

SEND NOTHING

GOOD (protect the planet, avoid potential offence caused by missing anyone off your analogue/digital Christmas card list)

— vs —

BAD (Branded a Grinch, Scrooge, etc... marginalized by friends, increasingly alone, sad, Zayn Malik).

Possible Solutions

❄ **Send a sustainable Christmas card:** Many physical, festive
cards still have glitter or other shiny elements that make them
hard/impossible to recycle – so swerve these. Instead, look for
cards with the Forest Stewardship Council (FSC) mark which
guarantees that the paper has been produced sustainably and
ethically. You can also buy 'plantable' cards, which feature
seeds (for veg and flowers) that you can sow in the spring.
After Christmas, recycle or compost your cards in the garden
– or, alternatively, cut them up and turn them into decorations
(or fun, festive jigsaw games for small children) for next year.

❄ **Turn a Christmas card into a Christmas ticket:** In terms of
cold, hard, brutal economics, this may not stack up if you have
friends or family members who live a great many miles away,
but... instead of spending your cash on a card and a stamp
to wish someone a merry Christmas, why not use the money
to buy a bus or train ticket, and go and say it in person. A
Christmas card is nice, but a Christmas hug is even nicer.

✻ **Return to sender:** This is an alternative way of recycling the cards you receive over the Christmas period. All it needs is a pen and quick reactions. As soon as a Christmas card comes through your letter box, open it, read it, enjoy the nice warm, fuzzy, festive feeling it elicits – then inside the card cross through *your* name in the 'Dear...' section, and the name of the sender in the 'Love from...' section, and rewrite them in the opposite places. Then quickly reseal the envelope, write 'return to sender' on the front, run out of the house and give the card back to the postman or woman, saying, *'Oops! One more for the Christmas post-bag, thanks!'* You can employ this same method when friends or family members physically hand you cards at Yuletide gatherings; tear open the envelope, swiftly read the lovely message inside, cross out and reverse the names, then hand the card straight back. It's possible you may get some surprised reactions – but the planet will thank you in the long run.

The Problem with Christmas Food (& Drink)

You might want to settle down somewhere comfy for this, there's a lot to say...

Christmas Is Coming... And It's Not Just The Goose Getting Fat.

Catering for Christmas is big business. Supermarkets and food manufacturers start thinking about *next* Christmas almost as soon as the bells have stopped jingling for this one.

As the new year dawns – and up and down the land, bloated men and women traipse unhappily into gyms and weight-loss classes, like fat zombies – teams of 'food futurists' and 'edibles engineers' are busily beavering away, trying to dream up and develop fantastical new ways to get even more calories into us next Christmas.

Food Scientist A:

'What about this...
We pump praline and
chicken liver parfait
inside chocolate "baubles"
dusted in edible gold,
which hang from the
antlers of a caramel-
coated Rudolph head –
complete with trillionaire
shortbread "brains" and
cherry ganache-glazed,
champagne truffle
"nose"...?'

Food Scientist B:

'It's good... but not
enough calories!'

A sure sign that Christmas is coming is the arrival of bizarre, new, 'Yuletide-themed' coffees advertised in the fake snow-frosted windows of Starbucks and its various rivals. If you've never tried a warm, steaming mug of 'roasted pumpkin & fireside slippers-flavoured latte' or a cream-covered maxi-venti-mega-cup of 'toffee & hazelnut mulledmochafrappafestive egganoggaccino', then save yourself the money and the 2,850 empty calories. They all taste a bit syrupy and sick-making.

'Yule LOVE This Eating Disorder!'

In these enlightened times, eating disorders like *anorexia* and *bulimia* are no longer stigmatized, and we feel better able to talk about them openly. However, there is a specific, insidious, holiday-related eating disorder that appears each December and grips the nation, but which no one seems to want to confront... It is *yuletidia gluttonia* – also known as 'feastive fever' or 'the merry madness'.

Most sensitive, switched-on contemporary people are aware of the dangers associated with overconsumption – be it of food or drink. Too much sugar can lead to obesity and diabetes. Too much alcohol can raise blood pressure and contribute to liver and heart disease. Too much of both can mean just one thing: *it's Christmas!*

There is an unwritten rule that, during the Christmas period, pretty much anything goes when it comes to food and drink. Normally sane, moderate people are transformed into ravenous, slobbering maniacs – especially during the days immediately after 25th December when there are 'leftovers' to be polished off. At this time, any amount of excessive or bizarre consumption can be excused with a wry smile and this simple phrase: 'It *is* Christmas after all.'

27 November

Husband: 'Fancy an omelette for breakfast?'

Wife: 'Thanks, but I'm trying to be good. I'll stick with muesli.'

27 December

Husband: 'Fancy an omelette for breakfast?'

Wife: 'Screw that. I'm having goose liver pâté on leftover yule log, washed down with a handful of Quality Street and a pint of Baileys Irish Cream liqueur.'

Let's Talk Turkey

Gobble, gobble – that's what Christmas is all about. Unless, of course, you're the poor, deceased turkey. It's now widely accepted that we need to rear and consume less meat if we want to try to slow down the terrible march of global warming. For the sake of our planet, and for future generations trying to forge some sort of meaningful life on this earth, we need to make changes right now. We need to turn our backs on meat and embrace a plant-based diet. But try telling that to Uncle Colin as he licks his greasy lips and tells you with wild, shining eyes, 'They've only gone and made chipolatas wrapped in *prosciutto* wrapped in *black pudding*! They call them pigs in eiderdowns!'

Christmas catering can be extremely challenging for the delicate, contemporary diner. Not only can the sheer excess of it all make you feel a bit queasy, but in most households meat is suddenly on display *everywhere*:

sausages wear little 'blankets' of bacon (in case they get cold in the oven?) or are rolled in flaky pastry, or fashioned into balls to be stuffed inside other unfortunate creatures bound for the roasting dish...

Duck, chicken, goose, wild boar, cockapoo – they can all be served up as anonymous-looking pâté... There's beef Wellington and boeuf bourguignon, veal and venison, honey-glazed ham and rack of lamb, dead-eyed smoked salmon and split-down-the-middle lobster thermidor... If you're especially unlucky, you might encounter an enthusiastic home cook who's decided to tackle a completely outmoded and needlessly complicated 'historic' dish, like a twelve-bird roast, which features ever-diminishing birds roasted one inside the other, like some kind of horrific Russian 'meat doll'.

But king of all of these burnt Yuletide offerings is the turkey (and what a spectacularly rubbish accolade that is – like being crowned the 'smelliest kid in school'). In Britain – even in these increasingly enlightened, sustainability-savvy times – an average of ten million turkeys are sold for Christmas. Ironically, after they've cooked and eaten a turkey, many Brits will complain that they didn't really like it and they found the meat too dry. It's a bit like going to a DIY store each Christmas, buying a new hammer, and then whacking yourself in the balls with it. As you shuffle towards the door, doubled over and wincing, you give the storekeeper a thumbs-up, and gasp: *'See you again, same time next year!'*

CALL-OUT CORNER
Christmas Turkeys

Poor old turkeys. Sure, they're not likely to get their own lucrative cosmetics campaign anytime soon, but is that any reason to fatten them up, chop off their heads and roast them for half the day? (If the answer were 'yes', you'd have to wonder what the future holds for Kim Kardashian...)

This Yule, instead of roast turkey, why not have a carbon-neutral nut roast (warning, to avoid possible allergic reactions, do <u>not</u> use nuts).

Possible Solutions

Navigating the Meat Minefield

❄ You could just turn up and say, *'Sorry, I was starving, so I've eaten already.'* Cooking at Christmas time for large groups of people is a notoriously stressful business – and kitchens are packed full of potentially deadly knives and assorted cooking implements – so use this excuse only if you are sure the chef is a patient, forgiving soul and not prone to sudden outbursts of extreme violence.

❄ If you're a vegetarian or a vegan planning to attend a festive feast at someone else's house, and you *aren't* hoping to spark a debate, then it may be a kindness to **contact your host in advance**, to make sure they know about your dietary choices and can plan accordingly. Or, alternatively, bring something with you that you know you can eat – and that other, interested guests could try if they're feeling veg-curious...

❄ Gently challenge whoever's doing the catering to **switch out some of those perennial, 'dirty', meat-heavy options for 'cleaner', plant-based alternatives.** Baby steps will do to begin with: no one has to trade out their precious roast bird for roast celeriac in year one, but there are countless delicious, inventive things you can do with veg – beyond boiling the life out of it – and the internet is packed with recipes and videos you could direct a loved one towards. Encourage them to operate a nightclub-style 'one in, one out policy': when a fresh, funky dish of twice-baked butternut squash with quinoa and Gorgonzola rocks up to the Yuletide table, maybe it's time to leave the pigs in blankets outside.

❄ If, however, you're a more politically minded plant-eater and you're spoiling for a fight, **bring a surprise guest with you. A turkey. A live one.** Give it a name, introduce it to everyone – *'Merry Christmas, everybody. This is my friend, Greg. He's a turkey'* – and insist it sits next to you at the table. *'Make room for Greg! It's his Christmas too – and he likes pulling crackers as much as I do.'* Even the most dedicated carnivore might pause for thought if they find themselves staring into the beady eye of a living turkey, while trying to tuck into a roasted one. (Plus, it's very hard to pull a cracker with someone if you've just sat opposite them and eaten their brother.)

In terms of the other festive excesses – the sweets and puddings, chocolate and cakes, cheese and biscuits, crisps and nuts, and all the MYRIAD TYPES OF BOOZE... Ultimately, you must find your own way through it all. It's like box-set bingeing: you have to decide how much you can stomach in any one sitting... But just in case, this Yuletide, a sweaty, grinning uncle – plate piled high with tasty titbits – nudges you in the ribs and says, 'Go on, live a little. It is Christmas after all!' here are a variety of potential responses you could offer, depending on your mood:

❄ 'As I strive to live lightly on the earth, so I try to graze lightly at the Christmas table.'

❄ 'You're right, but you know what they say: "A minute on the lips... morbid obesity, type 2 diabetes, increased risk of stroke, heart disease and cancer ".'

❄ 'Thanks, Uncle Steve, but I've reined back on the food and drink since last Christmas – when you 'pole danced' with the tree and then threw up on Grandma.'

The Problem with Family Gatherings

No one really wants to be alone at Christmas, but the alternative – the Big Christmas Family Get-Together – can be fairly daunting too.

A minority of people – the type with fridge magnets that say things like 'You call it chaos, we call it family!' – adore the excuse the festive season brings for relatives to spend time under the same roof.

But for many sane, well-adjusted men and women – especially younger adults who have previously flown the nest – the annual Christmas get-together can be the trigger for a multi-coloured spectrum of stresses, frustrations and anxieties. It makes a trip to the dentist look like a stroll through the park, with Jonathan Van Ness on one arm and Beyoncé on the other.

The central problem lies in the coming together of different generations. Even when the Avengers assemble, they don't always get on – and it's not like Iron Man's spouting outmoded ideas about equal pay for women, Thor's demanding to know 'Exactly what is vegan cheese?', and Captain America's making dubious jokes about whether it's better to fly or take the bus if he decides to go on a transgender 'journey'.

The Big Christmas Family Get-Together often takes place in an over-warm, physically and/ or emotionally claustrophobic environment – i.e. your family home. From the get-go, there's intense pressure to 'have fun' –

at almost any cost. If fun is *not* had, if people do *not* get on, then Christmas will be ruined (which is tantamount to poking Baby Jesus in the eye). The stakes are almost unbearably high...

This gathering of family members is the time when old stereotypes, tired tropes and troubling patterns of behaviour are likely to re-emerge – and when new beliefs, novel ideas and radical opinions will come under scrutiny and potentially face challenges and resistance – or worse, sarcasm. Chuck in a few bathtubs' worth of alcohol, simmering sibling resentments and the micro-aggressions associated with disappointing Christmas presents, and you've got the makings of a pretty special Yuletide powder keg...

Or, to put it another way: when families come together at Christmas, the shit often hits the festive fan.

How to navigate the minefield of festive family politics
(and actual politics)

※ How you get through Christmas with your family will largely depend on what kind of person you are, and how much you relish conflict. Some people – no matter how deeply held their personal beliefs – will take the **path of least resistance**, keep a low profile and try to get the whole thing done as quickly and with as little friction as possible. Others may just **'go Greta'** and broadcast their beliefs loudly, clearly and urgently at the Christmas table – whether that's telling Auntie Bev that she's married to a sexist misogynist dinosaur, or explaining to Grandpa that Brexit is far from 'over' – *'but it may be over for you soon because you're 83 and you've had your time and your fun and now you've royally f***ed it all up for the rest of us'.*

※ It's true that 'you can choose your friends, but you can't choose your family'. If you're lucky, though, you may get to **choose which members of your family you sit near** during the Christmas get-together. Choose the nicer, less provoking ones if you want to get through the day more easily. Put yourself in amongst the pricklier people if you want to make it a Christmas to remember…

❄ For the sake of peace and goodwill to all men, you could propose a **ban on divisive subjects** – politics, climate change, gender, sexuality, etc. – but there might not be much left to talk about over the Brussels sprouts, apart from celebrity gossip and speculation about whether there'll ever be another *Gavin & Stacey* Christmas Special (there will).

❄ Instead of creating a conversational wasteland, it might be better to try to **regulate the rules of engagement**. Like the feral boys in *Lord of the Flies*, who could only speak when they held 'the conch', why not nominate a festive object, a kind of 'Christmas conch', that can be passed around the room. This powerful Yuletide talisman will grant the person holding it an uninterrupted platform for their opinions – for a limited amount of time... *'Right, quiet everyone! Uncle Clive has got the Terry's Chocolate Orange – so, he's allowed to tell us exactly what he thinks about same-sex marriage for the next three minutes.'*

In Case Of Emergency...

Should you still need help to get through especially challenging right-wing dinner table conversations, pages 131 to 133 feature a variety of soothing images of **emotional support animals,** chosen for their ability to quell rage. If you find yourself teetering on the brink of unbridled fury, simply flick through these images, breathe deeply and slowly, and drink in their peace and balm.

Bottom line: blood is thicker than water. However heated the debate may get, no matter how much your younger brother winds you up, your patronizing aunt irritates you, your dad teases you, or your *Daily Mail*-quoting grandparents horrify you, they are all your family. Your tribe. You'll forgive them in the end – and they'll forgive you. And chances are you'll all be back again – same time, same place – next year.

The Problem with Christmas Party Games

You might think an effective way to dissipate the underlying tensions at the Big Christmas Family Get-Together would be to play a Christmas party game. But you'd be wrong.

Ironically, playing a Christmas party game could very well turn up the heat under the already bubbling festive pressure pot... Break out a 'fun game' and relatives who were just about managing to be civil around the dining table will soon feel unshackled, free to hurl abuse at one another, under the guise of playful 'party banter'.

Dip into a Yuletide family party during 'games time' and you'll almost certainly hear comments like these:

'OMG, Auntie Margaret! Did you REALLY not know that Copenhagen is the capital of Denmark? What are you, some kind of geographical MORON!?'

'PLEASE can we not have Uncle Simon on our Pictionary team? He draws like a drunk three-year-old!'

'For God's sake, Grandma, what the HELL are you doing?! You've just TOTALLY let them win, you absolute bell-end.'

Ten shocking, outmoded Christmas 'party games' that history would sooner forget...

From the Victorian era:

❄ Kick The Cat

❄ The Child Chimney Sweep Gets A Hot Bottom

❄ Is It Part Of The Empire?

❄ Yule Gruel!

❄ Pass The Lump Of Coal Without Using Your Hands

From the 1940s to the 1980s:

❄ This Christmas, I'll Be Giving Hitler...

❄ What Colour Am I?

❄ Photocopier Kiss Chase

❄ I'm Not A Fairy!

❄ Whose Breasts Are These?

Broadly speaking, Christmas party games break down into two categories:

1. **'Simple' games.** These generally require little or nothing in the way of equipment – boards, dice, counters, cards, etc. They are more likely to involve wordplay or acting (e.g. charades) or some kind of potentially embarrassing physical larks (e.g. limbo under a Christmas scarf).

2. **'I'll Explain The Rules' games.** This is the world of Trivial Pursuit, Monopoly, Cluedo, Articulate, Uno, Balderdash, Pictionary, etc. You'll need a table, pencils, scorecards, instructions, etc. And patience.

Generally, the people playing the Christmas party games can be divided into three types:

1. **Easy-going.** Does what it says on the tin. These are the folk who don't want to rock the Christmas boat. They're not that bothered about winning or losing, they're just happy to play along – they'll often be heard saying things like, '*It's a bit of harmless fun, it's not worth getting upset about.*' If festive gatherings were composed entirely of people like this, there would be less conflict at Christmas time, and fewer trips to A&E. But inevitably, that's not the case, because in amongst the Easy-going there will also be the...

2. **Competitive.** Again, the clue's in the name. These are the people who *pretend* it's all good, wholesome, light-hearted fun – but who secretly, fervently, wholeheartedly want to WIN. To win ABOVE ALL ELSE, whatever the cost. For these people, to lose – whether it's at Pictionary, Monopoly or Christmas scarf limbo – is to DIE INSIDE. A Competitive type can just about get along with an Easy-going type (as

long as they have a decent stab at playing the game) – but what he or she *cannot* tolerate, is the...

3. Confused. This person may be drunk ('It is Christmas after all!'), elderly, intellectually sub-optimal – or potentially all three of these things at the same time. You can easily identify the Confused type by their trademark cries and protests – for example:

> *'I don't UNDERSTAND! Will someone please EXPLAIN this game to me?!'*

> *'Wait a minute, whose team am I on? I think I've been moving the wrong piece.'*

> *'Well, this game's rubbish. I don't like it at all.'*

> *'The capital of Copenhagen? I have no idea. Is it Finland?'*

To avoid family-fracturing arguments, actual physical harm or all-out bloodshed, it may be wise to make sure that Competitive and Confused types do not end up on the same team – but it's often hard to orchestrate. Good luck.

Internet photo of a classic Christmas party game just moments before the violence breaks out.

CALL-OUT CORNER
Charades in the Post #MeToo Era

When it comes to party games, charades is a bona fide Christmas classic. For hundreds, maybe *thousands* of years, families have enjoyed the simple fun to be had in miming the name of a famous film, TV show, book or song.

Sadly, in light of the shameful abuses perpetrated by Hollywood movie mogul Harvey Weinstein, in the post #MeToo era there's a case for arguing that some films should no longer feature within charades – namely the ones that Weinstein had a hand in producing.

Notable titles to potentially avoid include: *The Lord of the Rings, Kill Bill, The English Patient, Shakespeare in Love, Finding Neverland, Spy Kids* and *Paddington*. For sensitivity's sake, you may want to redact them all.

Alternatively you could select a substitute film (perhaps a piece of independent art-house cinema) which tackles similar themes but is untainted by Weinstein's legacy. For example, instead of *Paddington* you could act out *Grizzly Man*, Werner Herzog's devastating and heart-rending documentary about the deadly perils of getting too close to cuddly creatures.

The Problem with Office Christmas Parties

When it comes to the Big Christmas Family Get-Together, a swirling mass of powerful emotions can compel a person to attend: amongst them might be love or longing, nostalgia, guilt, a sense of duty, the hope of reconnecting, or of receiving WHSmith vouchers... When it comes to the Office Christmas Party (OCP), the reasons for going tend to be more binary: if you do, it might be okay – if you don't, you run the risk of being branded a killjoy, or getting sacked.

Ironically though, by attending, you *also* run the risk of getting sacked.

Just as you can't choose your family members, so, by and large, you cannot choose your work colleagues. If you're lucky, you might have found friends and like-minded souls amongst them,

but there's no guarantee of this – especially in the fast-moving, modern world where men and women often work in silos (and earbuds), cut off from one another. Some people can go days, weeks or even months without really speaking to their colleagues – which, in part, is what makes the OCP so potentially fraught.

Apart from a fire drill, the OCP may well be the one time in the year when the usually disconnected assortment of co-workers has to down tools and spend any time genuinely together. The difference is, an efficiently run fire drill could be over in under ten minutes – the OCP could go on for many long hours. And instead of having to wait patiently by a lamp post as someone in a high-vis jacket crosses names off a register, you may have to wait patiently by a photocopier as someone in a novelty Christmas jumper tries to get off with you.

An HR Nightmare

In many ways the Office Christmas Party parallels the Big Christmas Family Get-Together: again, there's likely to be a gathering of different generations, many people will be there under duress or a sense of obligation, and there's that same slightly manic underlying pressure to *have fun*. However, status is now a factor too: at a family party, your boring Uncle Alan will almost certainly be older than you, and therefore feel entitled to lecture you about life – but it's unlikely he's also your line manager.

At the OCP, the usual lines of status are blurred, people on sometimes wildly different pay grades are suddenly thrown together, and obliged to interact. This could be uncomfortable, clunky, embarrassing... But, fortunately, humankind has invented something to help with that – and it is called ALCOHOL.

Alcohol: The Great Leveller?

Adding copious amounts of booze to the OCP fundamentally alters the dynamic. That same ragtag gang of people who, while sober, felt like they'd been assembled for an awkward team-bonding 'away day', are transformed – into the only survivors from a sinking ocean liner: raw, elemental, flesh-and-blood men and women thrown together in a fragile lifeboat, set perilously adrift in a raging sea. It's life or death. Who knows what tomorrow might bring, whether or not any of them will ever set eyes on their homes or loved ones again. Right now, in *this* moment, truths must be told, secrets must be shared, chests must be unburdened, opportunities must be seized. They MUST.

Common phrases you're likely to hear in the later stages of an Office Christmas Party (example names given purely for illustrative purposes – feel free to recast with people you may have encountered):

❈ 'You know, Suzy, you're a heck of a girl. I mean, woman. If I were twenty years younger, and not married with kids, I'd definitely try to snog your face off.'

❈ 'You know, Trevor, NO ONE fixes my internet issues like you do. People say you're weird, but as far as I'M concerned you are a 100%, solid-gold, freaking legend.'

❈ 'You know, Mr Jackson, the reason people are intimidated by you isn't because of your success. It's because of your breath. It's like a squirrel crawled into your mouth and died.'

Going Sober?

The OCP is a dangerous place. Many younger people have embraced clean living and choose not to 'poison themselves' with alcohol. You might think this would work in their favour...

Perhaps, instead of being caught up in the boozy madness, a sober Snowflake could spectate from the sidelines, like a visitor to the zoo, looking at the peculiar/frightening specimens kept safely behind toughened glass and wire fences?

In fact, being sober at an OCP can be counterproductive. The animals at this human zoo are not restrained by any kind of barrier – it's like *Jurassic Park* (the original and best one) from about twenty-seven minutes in, when it all goes to hell... In some ways – to avoid confusion, miscommunication and potential conflict – it might be better to be tipsy *with* your co-workers, so that you're in step with them, rather than out of kilter – like two people at a silent disco, one thrashing around to speed metal, the other drifting on a sea of acid jazz.

Power and Gender (and Karaoke)

Unfortunately, even though the normal lines of status are smudged at the OCP, chances are the same old power and gender dynamics will operate. It's not *impossible* that a younger, more junior woman will pin an older, more senior man up against the water dispenser and say, '*Oh my God, Graham! There's something about your middle-age spread, your sweaty armpits and your bald patch that's driving me WILD!*

Kiss me, you sexy bastard!' But it tends to happen a great deal less than middle-aged men would like to fantasize.

We can only hope that, in the future, as the workplace gender balance tips towards the horizontal, women will feel that they can, at last, sexually harass their male colleagues (especially their juniors) at the OCP. But chances are they won't bother – they'll probably just enjoy having a dance and a singalong to ABBA instead.

In the meantime, approach the OCP with care, try to hang out with the colleagues you like, maybe take a chance on those who look like they have a sense of humour, and do your best to avoid senior staff members with mistletoe sellotaped to their foreheads, lurking near the photocopier or water cooler.

Christmas Parties for One

It's worth sparing a thought for those freelancers and members of the 'gig economy' who don't get the chance to confront the challenges of an Office Christmas Party – because they work on their own, don't have any kind of physical office, or are employed by a business that would rather they were out delivering takeaways and cardboard boxes than attending a big, expensive party.

If you're one of these people, you can replicate an OCP in the comfort of your own bedroom: just turn down the lights, turn up the music, and have a drink or eleven. You *could* even sexually harass yourself, if the feeling takes you... no one need know and it avoids all the trauma of an employment tribunal.

A Word About 'Secret Santa'

People have been exchanging gifts at Christmas for a very long time, but 'Secret Santa' is a relatively new innovation – credited to an American entrepreneur and philanthropist called Larry Dean Stewart. Apparently, one especially harsh winter in 1979, kind-hearted Larry decided to start anonymously giving gifts of money to strangers who looked in need of help. It's estimated that the original 'Secret Santa' gave away more than $1.3 million over twenty-six years, before he sadly died, aged only fifty-eight.

Larry's heart was definitely in the right place, and he set a shining example with his quiet, covert acts of generosity. These days, however, 'Secret Santa' has moved on a bit. Instead of referring to a person – a kind of festive Clark Kent, who walks amongst us mere mortals, discreetly delivering Yuletide joy – Secret Santa is a *thing*, usually a thing that happens as part of an Office Christmas Party.

There are variations on how to 'do' Secret Santa in the workplace, but the basic idea is that a spending limit is fixed (e.g. £10), you draw a colleague's name randomly out of a hat, and then you have to buy them a gift for Christmas. So, it's entirely plausible that a poorly paid intern could be buying something for the boss, and vice versa.

As with Christmas party games, this sounds on the surface like it could be good, simple, light-hearted fun – but it very much depends on who's involved. Be warned, some people take the whole thing very seriously...

Scenario 1: Linda from Marketing and Bob from Sales

LINDA: 'Oh, you bought me a pack of Highland shortbread... How much did that cost?'

BOB: 'I dunno... about £4. Don't you like shortbread?'

LINDA: 'I do... But I spent £10 on an Argos voucher for Trevor the IT guy.'

BOB: 'Good for you. But the Secret Santa *limit* was £10. You didn't *have to* spend £10.'

LINDA: 'But I did.'

BOB: 'Well, more fool you.'

LINDA: 'Who are you calling a fool, you tight git?!'

BOB: 'Give me back my biscuits, you ungrateful cow!'

Scenario 2: Barbara from Accounts and Tina the new PA

BARBARA: 'Oh... you got me some skin cream. Thanks...'

TINA: 'Yeah, for your hands. Or your face.'

BARBARA: 'For my face? For my old, *wrinkled* face, you mean? Well, how great do I feel now? *"Happy Christmas, Barbara – you sad, wrinkled old bag."* Thanks, Tina, thanks a f***ing lot!'

Secret Santa can be a gift-giving minefield. Tread carefully, or turn to the **Problem with Gifts for Grown-Ups** chapter on page 37 for inspiration and alternative ideas.

The Problem with Santa

It was inevitable that we'd get round to this guy eventually. Santa Claus/Father Christmas/Old Nick/whatever you prefer to call him, is one of the big characters in the whole Yuletide show. Trying to talk about Christmas *without* referencing him is like trying to explain *Game of Thrones* without mentioning Jon Snow or Daenerys Targaryen, or all the gratuitous nudity. It's like trying to explain day without night, Ant without Dec... It can't be done.

There are a number of problems associated with Santa. Here, in no particular order, are some of the main ones...

SANTA: The Oppressor of Elves

Horrifyingly, people trafficking and human slavery persist in our modern world. All too often, there are stories in the news of people forced by debt or intimidation to become sex workers, cleaners, nail bar technicians... Most people with a conscience and a soul would maintain that it is totally unacceptable to coerce or compel others to work against their will for free. And yet, in all the reports of Santa and his 'merry band of elves', who has ever even once heard of these same apparently hard-working and skilled elves receiving a statutory minimum wage, holiday allowance or any kind of pension provision?

Like NATO weapons inspectors, you can go to Lapland in search of answers to these questions. You can visit 'the elves' workshop'; you may even be permitted to interact with a sweetly smiling, resolutely jovial elf. Chances are, if you ask, they will tell you they are 'happy' and 'well treated'. But if you try to dig any deeper, try to get behind the tight, fixed grin and the staring, 'joyful' eyes, they will invent some excuse – 'reindeer feeding' or 'gift wrapping' – and hurry away. Why? *Maybe*, because a reindeer is hungry or a toy needs packaging up... Or maybe because they are living in misery, forced to work around the clock – in pursuit of frankly outrageous

CALL-OUT CORNER
#SantaSoWhite

For as long as there's been a Santa, he's been an old white guy. If it wasn't for the splashes of red, he'd be an old white guy in a white costume with a hood – and that *really* isn't a good look... Surely, it's time for a 'reboot'. If Idris Elba does not get to play James Bond, then, by rights, he should get the Santa gig. He would be brilliant. Not only would Idris make a charming, charismatic and refreshingly contemporary Father Christmas – he'd also bring a smouldering intensity and an underlying sense of danger to the role, both of which have long been missing.

performance targets – by a tyrannical, chuckling slave driver.

SANTA:
The Bearded Barrier
to Equal Rights
for Women

We are led to believe that Santa Claus is a married man. Christmas films and children's cartoons focus almost exclusively on a male, Father Christmas-focused narrative – but they will often give us a brief glimpse of his wife in the wings. Generally, she is portrayed as a big-hearted, good-natured, fairly long-suffering help-mate to Santa, usually to be seen bustling about with a broom or lamenting the fact that her husband is so busy and preoccupied with all the list-writing, reindeer-wrangling, gift-giving, etc...

Santa's wife is a cipher. There's nothing to her. If this was a TV show, she would be a criminally underwritten character. We don't even know her name. Is she Sue Claus? Caroline? Desirée? No one knows – because no one seems to care. Sometimes, she's called 'Mother Christmas' – and yet she seems to have no children of her own. So, in a way, that's a cruel joke: a name given to a woman who has a small army of peculiar, enslaved, elf 'children', but no offspring of her own. This poor, barren, nameless woman is married to one of the most famous men in the world – but does he do anything to raise her up, to give her a platform of her own, to share his fame or his career with her?

Ho, ho, no.

We cannot know for certain that Santa has been gaslighting Sue/Caroline/Desirée Claus, but it seems wholly plausible. It's not hard to imagine him telling her, *'It's kind of you to offer to help me deliver the presents, but you get a bit nervous around the reindeer, don't you? And, let's be honest, you're not the best sleigh driver. And, don't forget, you get a bit funny around children. I think it's probably best that you stay at home, don't you? You could do a bit of sweeping up with your broom, and look after the elves – they think of you as a mother... Lovely "Mother Christmas"... What's that? No, don't be silly, people don't need to know your actual name. You've got a name. You're Mrs Santa Claus. You're my wife. What more does anyone need to know?'*

This Yuletide, spare a thought for Mrs Christmas.

SANTA: The Genetic Engineer Gone Mad

Five words: Rudolph the Red-Nosed Reindeer.

Not only does this poor creature have an unnatural, red-coloured, sometimes shiny, sometimes glowing nose, he can *fly*. And, because he can fly, Rudolph and his bizarrely named reindeer companions are also kept in bondage, forced – like the poor, put-upon elves – to do Santa's bidding. Namely, to pull a heavy,

almost certainly overloaded (**#healthandsafetygonemad**) sleigh *around the world*, throughout the night – with no break. Even an Amazon worker gets a three-minute 'rest stop' every five hours/6,000 packages shipped. Rudolph and Co. are essentially antler-wearing Deliveroo drivers, without even a zero-hours contract...

SANTA: The Joe Exotic of Lapland (aka the 'Reindeer King')

Along with Rudolph everyone's heard of Dasher, Dancer, Prancer and Vixen, Comet, Cupid, Donner and Blitzen. But what about the tenth Christmas reindeer, Fetlocks of Fury, who sprained an ankle on his maiden flight and was never seen or heard of again? With his jolly laugh, twinkly eyes and lovely, long, curly white beard, Santa doesn't *seem* like the sort of person who could deliver a karate death-chop to the frail, unsuspecting neck of an injured reindeer, then butcher, barbecue and eat him on Boxing Day – but where did that noble beast go…? Only Santa and the nine remaining reindeer know. Would *you* talk if you were one of them?

SANTA:
The Stranger Who
Breaks Into Your Home

In modern, Western society, we have become obsessed with paedophiles. We see them everywhere. Like pigeons. Only these pigeons are terrifying, sinister and should be locked up. Just a few generations ago, British children lived in a charmed, paedophile-free world, where they could play unsupervised in the streets and wander off by themselves – spying on foreign types who might be up to no good, camping out in the woods, poking unexploded World War II bombs with sticks – and no one thought twice about it, least of all their pipe-smoking, drunk-driving, non-seatbelt-wearing parents.

These days, that's all changed. Now we understand (thanks in no small part to the *Daily Mail*) that paedophiles are *all around us*. Like squirrels. Only they're not as obvious and flagrant as squirrels. They're more like badgers. This is why the *Daily Mail* hates both paedophiles and badgers.

Unlike the Victorians – who either closeted their children away with paid strangers in creepy nurseries or stuffed them up chimneys – enlightened, modern parents keep their children shielded from the dark forces in the world, telling them to be suspicious of strangers, and on no account to accept gifts from them.

So, how incredibly WEIRD, confusing and contradictory then, that when Christmas rolls round, these same over-protective parents tell their children that, if they are *lucky*, an elderly man – who has been *spying* on them, *closely monitoring their behaviour at all times* – will come creeping down the chimney in the dead of night, and will tiptoe around their house, perhaps even in their bedrooms. No one needs worry about *this* bearded, nocturnal stranger, carrying gifts, though... Not because he's been CRB checked, but because he's good old Santa. It's no wonder children can't get to sleep on Christmas Eve. It's not excitement keeping them awake – it's pure, unadulterated fear.

TIMMY: 'Mummy, didn't you say there are bad people in the world, and that's why we lock the door at night and turn on the burglar alarm?'

MUM: 'Yes, darling, that's right. We don't want strangers in our house. Clever you for remembering! Now into bed now. And no nonsense. Don't forget, Santa's watching you! He's watching *everything you do*.'

TIMMY: 'Like a paedophile, Mummy?'

MUM: 'Oh no, nothing like a paedophile.'

TIMMY: 'Is he a burglar then, Mummy?'

MUM: 'No, he's not a burglar, more like a home invader. But a lovely one. As long as you've behaved. Goodnight!' (closes door)

TIMMY: (cries)

A Santa for the Twenty-First Century?

These are just a few of the most obvious problems relating to Santa. There are others – (e.g. his self-defined code of what is 'naughty' and what is 'nice', his questionable kissing of children's mummies underneath the mistletoe *despite* being a married man, his lucrative association with a well-known brand of sugary, fizzy drink... the list goes on) – but the Santa that we know has been forged over *many* years.

As long as there are rumours that Idris Elba could be the next James Bond, there's hope that, one day, Father Christmas – the overweight, elderly white man with the tokenistic wife – will be depicted as a happy, healthy woman of colour, who is in a loving, equal-status, polyamorous relationship with another woman and a trans person. The three of them have liberated the elves, returned the reindeer to the wild and done away with gift-giving on 25th December – encouraging everyone to shake a stranger by the hand, and do one kind deed instead.

It *might* happen. If we all made enough noise, marched in the streets, signed a petition... Idris might get his shot, and Santa might get a wake-up call.

It's the least we can do for Fetlocks of Fury.

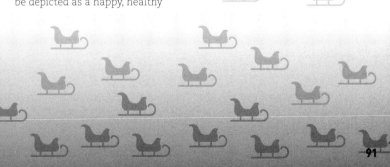

The Problem with Snow

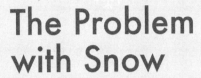

As hard as Bing Crosby, Michael Bublé and assorted other crooners might dream of a *white* Christmas, there's no guarantee that we'll get one. In fact, thanks to the climate crisis and global warming, it seems less and less likely. Moving forward, it might be more appropriate if Michael sang *'I'm dreaming of a mildly temperate Christmas, without freak storms, hurricanes or other extreme weather conditions – and all the environmental damage and human suffering that they bring...'* but he probably won't (to be honest, as lyrics go, it's not massively earwormy – though David Guetta or Calvin Harris could possibly do something with it...).

If there is a cold snap around 25th December, Bing's wish might come true – and we could actually get a white Christmas. On the plus side, this would probably be very pretty. Snow on the rooftops can be very attractive – it's a look Phillip Schofield has been rocking very successfully for a number of years now...

But – aside from all the travel delays and disruption, the increased pressure on the emergency services and the additional risk to the elderly and the homeless – there are other significant snow-related issues to think about. Ironically, for a Snowflake, there are serious ethical problems associated with snowflakes.

Frosty the Snowman: Another Pale Stale Male

Until box office mega-smash *Frozen* gave the world the wise-cracking, unfeasibly cute, singing snowman 'Olaf', the imaginatively named 'Frosty' was probably the most famous snowman in modern culture. His only near rival was the (even less imaginatively named) 'Snowman' from *The Snowman* – the illustrated children's book which spawned a cartoon and a hit Christmas song, which in turn catapulted Aled Jones to fame and ultimately paid for his conservatory, his swimming pool and his lovely white 'teeth'.

It's not Frosty's fault, or the Snowman's, or even Olaf's – but between them they stand together as a grinning, happy-go-lucky, carrot-nosed, twiggy-armed, pipe-smoking symbol of something far more sinister and troubling: namely, a deeply ingrained, widely accepted sexism.

Why snow*man*? Why not, snow*woman*? (Or snow*oman*, even?)

In most countries across the planet, the female share of the population stands at approximately 49 to 51 per cent – but when was the last time you saw a snowwoman? Have you *ever* seen one? The disturbing truth is you stand a better chance of seeing Donald Trump selling vegan chocolate brownies door-to-door to raise money for Greenpeace, than you do of laying eyes on this 'unicorn' of the snow-based sculpture world.

5'5" [1]   [2]   [3]   5'5"
5'0"   5'0"
4'5"   4'5"
4'0"   4'0"
3'5"   3'5"
3'0"   3'0"
2'5"   2'5"

Why? It's not like there are any specific 'rules' to making a snowman. It's just a given, that if it snows, and you build a 'person' out of that chilly, white stuff – it's a 'he'. Even Olaf's buddies Elsa and Anna do it unquestioningly – and they're pretty switched-on to women's equality, solidarity in sisterhood, and generally positive attitudes and behaviours. **#FrozenFangirl, #LetItGoRulez, #OMGIntoTheUnknown**

This Christmas, if it snows, instead of building a snowman, break with convention – and build a snow*woman* instead. Or, perhaps, build one of each. They could be shaking hands, high-fiving or holding a home-made banner that reads: 'JUST SAY S**NO**W TO SEXISM.'

Of course, even this proposition doesn't truly reflect the world we live in today. It's too binary, too simplistic and limiting to say that there can be either snow*men* or snow*women*, and that's it. You may identify as a different gender from the 'sex' you are assigned at birth – in fact, you may make the brave choice to change your 'sex' to reflect that powerful, inner voice. In the twenty-first century, we can be male, female, indeterminate or intersex – and why should we deny that same spectrum of choice to snow folk?

If you want to be truly sensitive next time it snows, build a snowman, and a snowwoman, and a snow*person*. Or, to go a step further, you could simply sculpt a large heap of snow into a non-specific shape – be careful not to make it phallic – and leave it on display as a gesture of your rejection of the old, outmoded ways…

Snowball Fights

Once upon a time, when people knew no better, they told themselves that snowball fighting was good, clean, wholesome fun. Of course now we can see it for what it is: encouraging and enabling aggression via 'weaponized snow'.

There is already more than enough violence and hostility in the world. No one ever forged a brave new friendship or ended a bitter, cross-border conflict by chucking a snowball in someone else's face, or – worse still – at the back of their head.

No one ever felt that cold, stinging *thwack*, or the horrific, icy trickle down the back of their neck, and thought, 'Thank you for that, brother, sister... Your well-aimed snowball has brought me to my senses and filled my heart with love.' They just thought, 'Jesus Christ! You little shit! I'm gonna kill you!'

If a child you know suggests a snowball fight, you'll be doing them a service if you gently but firmly refuse – and instead, sit them down, and tell them in no-holds-barred detail about the bloody horrors of war.

All conflict starts somewhere, and if no more snow was thrown in anger, arguably, this would be a safer, gentler, better world.

The Problem with Christmas Music

Slade's 'Merry Xmas Everybody', Wizzard's 'I Wish It Could Be Christmas Everyday', Shakin' Stevens' 'Merry Christmas Everyone'... depending on your musical tastes, you'll either think that Christmas music is jolly, festive fun – or that it's an annual human rights violation. Either way, it's pretty much unavoidable.

In the UK, there are no actual rules or government guidelines about when radio DJs can begin playing Christmas music, but it's usually wall-to-wall Wizzard from 1st December through to year end. It's hardly surprising that Slade frontman Noddy Holder refers to December as 'The Money Month' – or that Mariah 'All I Want For Christmas' Carey calls it 'The Golden Time'.

The Pogues' 'Fairytale of New York' has proved such a perennial Christmas favourite, that eccentric lead singer Shane McGowan – who recorded the lyrics with the late Kirsty MacColl back in 1987 – stopped working many years ago. Apparently, he also stopped paying for things in the way that normal people would.

Famously, the Queen doesn't carry money – and, rumour has it, neither does Shane. In the 359 days leading up to 25th December, instead of handing over physical money in exchange for food, clothes, fuel, toilet roll, all the usual stuff – Shane scribbles the message: *'IOU – Shane McGowan. Don't you worry… Christmas is coming!'* on a Post-it note, sticks it to the forehead of the till operator, and skips merrily out of the shop.

A Fairytale of Verbal Abuse

Ironically, 'Fairytale of New York' is the Christmas song most likely to cause problems and/or embarrassment to a sensitive, contemporary listener. Probably less thanks to Shane's drunken, slurring delivery (though that might play a part) – and more because of its use of a slang term that was fairly offensive in 1987 but is eye-wateringly repugnant

in 2020. It's not a word that needs to be printed here – in a book that promotes sensitivity and acceptance – but, if you've somehow not heard the song (perhaps you were raised by an isolated tribe living deep in the Brazilian rainforest), it rhymes with 'maggot' and starts with an 'f'.

If this particular f-word offends you (and if you're reading this book, chances are it *will*), it's best to be on 'Fairytale' standby throughout the Christmas period. Even if you choose not to listen to the radio, it will be hard to travel in a lift, or shop anywhere during December, without hearing Shane and Kirsty slinging lyrical abuse at one another every ten minutes or so. Here's what to do…

When Kirsty sings the phrase *'You scumbag, you maggot'*, drop everything, and put your fingers in your ears for a slow, steady count to five. Or, if there's a child nearby, drop everything, put your fingers in *their* ears, and shout 'DING DONG MERRILY ON

An Alternative
Yuletide Playlist

❄ Last Christmas
(If We Don't Do Something About Climate Change)

❄ All I Want For Christmas Is You To Stop Flying
(Alternative B-Side: *All I Want For Christmas Is Glue*)

❄ Greta, Baby

❄ I Wish It Could Be The UN Climate Change
Conference Every Day

❄ Green Christmas

❄ Driving Home For Christmas In My Electric Car

❄ Baby, It's Not Cold Enough Outside

❄ Silent Trump

❄ Walking In The Air Instead Of Flying

❄ Rockin' Around The Ethically Grown
Sustainable Christmas Tree

HIGH! IN HEAVEN THE BELLS ARE RINGING!' Try to smile as you shout, if you can, so as not to alarm the youngster. When the danger has passed, remove your fingers, pat them on the head and send them on their way.

A Musical Minefield

'Fairytale' isn't the only hit in the Christmas canon that raises issues... Other Christmas 'classics' have come under fire in recent years, due to what are now perceived to be dubious lyrics or questionable messages: 'Baby It's Cold Outside' has been accused of sinister, coercive/sexually aggressive undertones... Some feminists are unimpressed that all strong, independent, modern woman Mariah Carey wants for Christmas is a man... There's no doubt Michael Jackson was a musical genius, but he was also a deeply troubled soul, and it's been suggested that the trauma of singing 'I Saw Mommy Kissing Santa Claus' over and over again to millions of people as a child might have contributed to some

of his subsequent mental health issues... We'll never know.

This Yule, if one of the Christmas 'danger songs' comes on, either resort to the fingertips method outlined above or, if appropriate, crisply and clearly say the phrase, *'Alexa, skip!'*

The fact is, recording a catchy Christmas hit is the holy grail for many a musician. Elton's done it. Macca's done it. Cliff's done it. Bing did it. Bublé keeps on doing it. It's the musical equivalent of winning the lottery, every year. It's a pension. Who can blame the musos for having a go? In a similar spirit, the author of this book would like to offer up the following lyrics for a fresh, festive, Snowflake-friendly spin on a Christmas classic. If Gary Barlow, Sia or will.i.am fancy getting this hit recorded and in the download charts, they should feel free to contact the publishers as soon as possible...

'THE SNOWFLAKE SONG'
(to be sung to the tune of Shakin' Stevens' 'Merry Christmas Everyone')

Snow is melting
All around us
Planet's warming
That's no good.

Join the snowflakes,
It's time to make some changes
Stop buying plastic,
And eat plant-based food.

Greta's coming
To kick some asses,
But she can't do it,
All by herself.

Be like the snowflakes,
Hire a tree this Christmas
Make your own gifts,
And free the elves.

There's gonna be a rebellion
tonight,
I'm gonna glue myself,
To a turkey farmer's Land Rover
And give him a festive fright!

This December,
Build a snowperson,
Gender-neutral
Just as fun.

Be like the snowflakes
Full of love and understanding
Sensitive and caring
Just like Gok Wan.

There's gonna be a rebellion
tonight, etc...

THE TWELVE DAYS OF CHRISTMAS

Rebooting a Yuletide 'favourite' for the modern age

There are a number of reasons why the phrase 'Let's sing "The Twelve Days of Christmas"!' might fill a person with dread. Not only is this one of the most time-consuming, energy-sapping, teeth-itchingly irritating festive anthems, it also promotes an unhealthy and distinctly troubling message: one of mass consumption and greed.

Musical scientists equipped with powerful calculators (and great wells of patience) have worked out that the 'true love' referred to in the song hands over a total of 364 gifts to the gloating 'me'. By anyone's standards, that is an obscene amount of presents, a shameful drain on resources – as well as calling birds, French hens and turtle doves.

This Yuletide, if someone you know utters those dreadful words, 'Let's sing "The Twelve Days of Christmas"!', why not remind them that we are in the throes of a global climate crisis and suggest that if they *must* sing TTDOC then they replace the old, outmoded words with these new, eco-sensitive, switched-on lyrics...

1.

On the first day of Christmas,
My true love gave to me,
A sustainable Christmas tree.

2.

On the second day of Christmas,
My true love gave to me,
Two bags for life,
And a sustainable Christmas tree.

3.

On the third day of Christmas,
My true love gave to me,
Three big hugs,
Two bags for life,
And a sustainable Christmas tree.

And so on... through to verse twelve:

12.

On the twelfth day of Christmas,
My true love gave to me,
Twelve snowflakes singing
Eleven rioters rebelling,
Ten turkeys thriving,
Nine schoolkids striking,
Eight millennials marching,
Seven snowpeople smiling,
Six vegans vegging,
Five recycled things,
Four home-made gifts,
Three big hugs,
Two bags for life,
And a sustainable Christmas tree.

(Author's note: if you manage to sing that all the way through, well done, and thank you – now have a lie down, you deserve it.)

The Problem with Christmas TV

Chances are you'll find you watch a lot of TV over the Christmas period – especially if you end up in the intense, festive 'family bubble' for those jingle-fuelled days between Christmas Eve and the new year. Watching somebody else's unfolding drama may provide a welcome respite from whatever story's playing out in your own domestic Yuletide 'precinct'.

Once upon a time, the issue of what to watch at Christmas was potentially as divisive and incendiary as any chat about politics, climate change or gender. In the dark days before laptops, tablets, smartphones, Netflix, Apple TV, YouTube, Facebook et al – when there were perhaps only four or five channels, and one or two TVs in the house – the battle for who had sovereignty over the remote control could be as fierce and bloody as any episode of *Game of Thrones*.

Nowadays, it's entirely plausible that a multi-generational family could be sitting in the same room at Christmas, all watching entirely different things simultaneously – which, in a way, is a little tragic. So perhaps this Yule, you should suggest to your family that you go 'old school' – set aside the devices, huddle up on the sofa and watch something together.

But what to watch...?

Just as there are food scientists working from January onwards to devise ever more elaborate ways to fill us with Christmas calories, so there are legions of TV types, in oversized media glasses with asymmetrical beards and dazzling white trainers, frantically dreaming up festive-themed programming.

The Christmas Special

At its most basic, this will often mean adding some combination of the words 'Christmas', 'Christmas Special', or 'At Christmas' to a show's normal title, to inject a bit of festive fun – for example: *Christmas Antiques Roadshow*, *Crimewatch – Christmas Special*, and *Snapped: Women Who Kill – At Christmas*. These are existing TV formats given a sprinkling of Yuletide sparkle: the presenters might wear a jolly hat or comedy jumper and the theme tune might have been pimped up with a few sleigh bells. It's relatively harmless stuff.

The Christmas Cash-in

Then there are the programmes specifically invented *for* Christmas. In the 'non-scripted' realm (i.e. anything that isn't a drama), this will inevitably mean a smorgasbord of festive food and cookery shows. Across the channels you'll see the nation's favourite TV foodies battling it out – desperate to share their 'Christmas secrets' and show you the best ways to roast a turkey so that it stays 'lovely and moist'.

It would be wrong to accuse *all* television of being cynical and manipulative – but the truth is, as soon as those same bearded, trainer-wearing TV types have got their Christmas food shows commissioned, they start busily inventing 'healthy living, guilt-inducing, time-to-turn-over-a-new-leaf-you-fat-slob' formats ready to be broadcast just days later, in the new year.

Mary Berry: *'This is a bit of a secret, but I like to cook the turkey on a medium heat for 26 hours, then call the local fire brigade to put it out – that way it stays lovely and moist.'*

Heston Blumenthal: *'This year, I've decided to do something a bit special and cook the turkey in the deep end of a swimming pool – so that it stays lovely and moist.'*

23 December, 7 p.m., ITV

John Torode's Christmas Blowout

'Welcome to my Christmas banquet! It's gonna be a feast of festive food. I ho-ho-hope you're hungry!'

3 January, 10 a.m., ITV

Joe Wicks' New Year Workout, featuring John Torode

'Welcome to my new year's weight-loss boot camp! It's gonna be intense! I hope you're ready to sweat! You and this famous fatty.'

The Christmas Countdown Show

Another seasonal TV invention is the festive list show – a mammoth Christmas countdown of some fairly arbitrary subject, given a Yuletide spin. Inevitably, these shows – which will often run for many long hours, sometimes whole days – will feature a conveyor belt of comedians and minor celebrities either explaining what's *about* to happen in a clip, or reflecting on what *just* happened in a clip: TV loves them. Here are a few that will almost certainly be coming to your festive family get-together soon:

* ❄ The Top 100 Christmas Cat Clips

* ❄ The Nation's Favourite Christmas Crisp Flavours

* ❄ When Christmas Trees Attack – aka It Shouldn't Happen To A Celebrity/Reality TV Star At Christmas

* ❄ Jingle Smells: Britain's 50 Favourite Festive Fragrances

* ❄ Carol's Carols: Carol Vorderman Counts Down the UK's 300 Favourite Christmas Carols.

The Period Drama

Christmas is traditionally a good time for a big period drama – often a Dickensian adaptation or something by Jane Austen or Agatha Christie. On the surface, these lavish affairs can be good, family fun – but you should be braced for a fairly shocking lack of diversity, gender imbalance that makes *Mad Men* look positively cutting-edge, slavery, an almost total absence of workers' rights, domestic and child abuse, corruption, poverty, illness, violence, untimely death, and a lot of weird dancing. You might want to re-watch the *Gavin & Stacey Christmas Special* instead.

The Soap Opera

It's been established elsewhere in this guide that Christmas is a time for EXCESS – and nowhere is that more true than in the world of TV soap operas. If you find yourself settling down with your gran to watch one of the big soaps – whether it's set in a bustling corner of London's East End, or a quiet, farming community in the Yorkshire dales – just do so with your eyes wide open. Know, as the familiar opening credits come to their end, that this is Christmas, and in Soap Land, at Yuletide, ANYTHING GOES.

Rumour has it that, as December approaches, the writers of these soaps are locked in windowless rooms under the BBC, ITV and Channel 4 for days at a time. An endless loop of Christmas pop tunes and carols is piped in via hidden speakers. For sustenance, they are provided with only a vast mound of mince pies and sausage rolls, and given nothing to drink but gallons and gallons of potent, boozy eggnog... It's in this feverish, festive state that they will conceive their most fantastical and ludicrous Yuletide plot twists, the improbable surprises and spectacular stunts, the apocalyptic disasters and Christmas calamities...

If you don't relish watching a pub full of happy, carolling Cockneys being blown apart by an explosion of trapped sewer gasses from a monster 'fatberg', or seeing a jolly Yuletide barn dance turn into blood-soaked chaos as the giant blades of a nearby wind turbine break free of their moorings and come crashing down a hillside – then, sensitive reader, a Christmas visit to Soap Land may not be for you.

Schmaltzy Christmas Movies

Not *all* Christmas movies are cloying, gooey schmaltz fests, where improbable, two-dimensional characters get into ridiculous/'hilarious' scrapes at embarrassing family get-togethers, a promising romance gets derailed, for a while it looks like Christmas will be a total write-off, but then, finally everything gets sorted out in some fairly ludicrous way, and the vanilla, heterosexual hero and heroine have a snog in the snow… But quite a lot of Christmas movies *are* like that. By and large, these films are harmless enough, and if you're amongst family at Christmas telly time you may not want to rock the boat. But just remember, you can never *unwatch Love Actually*.

The Queen's Speech

Depending on their feelings towards the monarchy, that same elderly, soap-loving relative might insist that you sit down to watch the Queen's Speech. In case you've never tuned in for this rip-roaring roller-coaster ride, be warned – the Queen's Speech has nothing to do with RuPaul. Instead, TQS is essentially an annual, extended status update from the original Queen – Her Majesty, the Queen. From the comfort of one of her large private residences (**#AirBNoThankYouVeryMuch**), HRH reflects on what's been going on in the world in the past year, glosses over the unfortunate, headline-grabbing scrapes her own family have got themselves into, and never – not once – reveals her Christmas secret for roasting a swan so that it stays 'lovely and moist'.

In fairness to the Queen – who still looks amazing, really, considering how old she is (**#NoFillerNeededWith-GenesLikeThese**) – Her Majesty does try to be fairly switched-on to contemporary global affairs. She's unlikely to punch the air and shout 'Go Greta!' or actually say 'Donald Trump is a f***ing w***er' – but you get the sense she knows what's going on… Sadly – because she is a lot more aware than many other ninety-somethings – it means her annual address to the nation is usually a long list of all the worst, darkest, most upsetting

and anxiety-inducing things that have happened to the world in the past twelve months – generally ending with a kind of *'Hey ho! Stiff upper lip and all that. Onwards and upwards!'* vibe. With this in mind, you should probably watch TQS with a box of tissues in one hand and a stress ball in the other.

Alternatively, instead of listening to the reflections of one of the world's wealthiest, white, upper-class OAPs, you could do something more democratic, and arguably more 'real'…. This Christmas, why not knock on a neighbour's door and ask their grandma to stand framed in a front window and talk at you for a few minutes about what's been going on…

'…Then our Gary got a promotion! Head of branch, we're very proud!… I won £50 at the bingo, so that was good – but then the doctor said I need hip replacement surgery, so that was bad… I can't stay long, it's the Corrie Christmas Special tonight – they've just opened a nuclear power plant in Weatherfield, I don't think that's gonna end well…'

The Christmas Ads

Ironically, in the UK, one of the most eagerly anticipated Christmas TV moments is not actually a programme in its own right – it's an advert, for the department store John Lewis. Generally, these ads tell a brief, heart-warming tale, usually featuring themes of friendship and generosity, accompanied by a contemporary chart-topper performing a slowed down, stripped back version of an old, forgotten pop song. Pretty much anything goes when it comes to these musical mash-ups: Bastille covered 1985 hit 'Can't Fight This Feeling'… The Vaults did their version of 1980s 'One Day I'll Fly Away'… Rumours have it that, this Christmas, it will be a gently strummed acoustic guitar and Billie Eilish sing-whispering *'I like big butts and I cannot lie'* from 1992's rap classic 'Baby Got Back'.

At its most basic level, advertising promotes consumption, and you may feel that the John Lewis ads are nothing more than the cynical exploitation of an array of cute, computer-generated creatures – dragons, bears, hares, penguins, etc. – to shift more product. But even if it is just an elaborate ploy to sell more socks, it's only two and half minutes of your life, and the John Lewis ad will almost certainly be less traumatizing than most of the other offerings in the Yuletide TV schedules. If it was the *only* thing you watched this Christmas, you might feel you'd got off lightly.

An Alternative to Christmas TV...

If reading all of the above makes you want to turn your back on TV this Christmas, why not read a book instead? You've nearly got to the end of this one, and there are tons more to enjoy – free of talking-head comedians, endless countdowns and pushy commercials.

Author's note: John Lewis tried to negotiate ad space within this guide – three pages halfway through, telling the story of a cute Christmas hedgehog who is accidentally run over and then nursed back to health by an attractive, blended, modern family (to the strains of Lewis Capaldi covering Black Lace's 'Agadoo' in the audiobook version) – but the author and publishers stood their ground. Christmas should NOT be about consumption (apart from consumption of this book, obvs).

The Problem with New Year's Eve

You've made it through Christmas. You've survived the office party and the various family gatherings. You've given out eco-friendly cards and gifts, avoided the mounds of meat, swerved the sugary Christmas coffees, said a polite but firm 'no' to carol singers and snowball slingers, built a gender-neutral snowperson, navigated the minefield of boozy relatives wanting to pick a fight over politics, sex and sustainability, played censored charades and managed to pull not even one crappy cracker...

Congratulations. The end is in sight. But there's one last event in the Yuletide calendar that needs crossing off... New Year's Eve.

For Snowflakes and Noflakes alike, the main issue with New Year's Eve is the same, and a familiar one from the whole Christmas period: it is the pressure to have FUN.

On the surface, Christmas Day and New Year's Eve look pretty similar – like a leopard and a cheetah. Both are large, spotty cats whose whiskers you should not pull, but they are actually different – and so it is with these two big dates in the run-up to year's end.

Both will usually involve the coming together – sometimes

reluctantly – of large groups of family members and friends (some of them secretly slightly astonished that here they are again, with the same people, replaying the same conversations and indulging in the same excesses and activities – like getting caught in a Christmassy glitch in *The Matrix*).

At both events there will be food in abundance, and often a lot of strong drink too. Music is likely to be played, and so might board games. At both, crackling in the background like a log fire, will be the tension that comes when a large group of people are obliged to 'have fun'.

But if Christmas Day is a sprint, New Year's Eve is a marathon. That's the whole point. Turn up for lunch on 25th December and you might be able to beat a respectable retreat by early evening – but if you rock up to NYE celebrations, you're there for the long haul. It's an unspoken rule: no one's going anywhere until the fat lady sings. Specifically, until she sings 'Auld Lang Syne', a song with lyrics dating back to 1788 that NO ONE today actually knows or understands. We see the Queen make a speech on Christmas Day, so why don't we see her singing 'Auld Lang Syne' with the rest of the nation on New Year's Eve? Because even she, at her great age, doesn't know the words and couldn't tell you what they meant. No one can.

NB: If ever you meet the Queen, do NOT bring this up – as it could be deemed an act of treason, and see you thrown in the Tower for life.

Countdown to #Christpleaseletthis-beoversoon...

Most sensible, sensitive souls will take to their bed before midnight on 31st December, tucked up, listening to a soothing podcast about sustainability, buds in tight to block out the nonsense dronings of 'Auld Lang Syne'.

If not, as well as having to face the ordeal of hour upon hour of 'forced fun', they must also, finally, confront 'The Countdown'.

No one *really* enjoys a countdown. (Unless it's 'The Final Countdown' by eighties rockers Europe – and even that's a matter of musical taste.) If you work for NASA – in launch control or as a brave astronaut – as you listen to those numbers ticking inexorably down, you're probably wondering if your rocket's about to go up or blow up. Either way, it's a scary prospect.

By and large, countdowns tend to signify scary prospects. In the delivery room, you'll rarely hear a midwife counting down *'Five... four... three... two... one... It's a girl!'* It's the same at weddings, the officiating minister almost never calls out, *'Three ... two... one... You may kiss the bride!'*

When we hear a countdown, we're programmed to think something pretty explosive is going to happen on zero – maybe even an actual explosion. Definitely something momentous. But the truth about The Countdown to New Year's Eve is that, after Big Ben strikes twelve, not much does happen.

No one wants to hear a countdown that goes: *'Ten... nine... eight... seven... six... five... four... three... two... one... Anticlimax!'*

We want our explosion. But – because it wouldn't be practicable, sensible or advisable to detonate actual explosives in our major cities each 31st December – the fireworks we're anticipating have been moved 500 feet up into the air, and turned into actual fireworks.

Fireworks: A Traumatic Tradition

As any cowering golden retriever, fearful fox or bewildered badger will tell you, fireworks may look very pretty, but they are also very noisy, frightening and upsetting. Detonating millions of pounds worth of snazzy, sparkly, multi-coloured ordnance high overhead may be a pretty way of welcoming in the new year – but it's not especially kind to our furry friends. Arguably, the money that gets spunked up in the sky could have been better spent on propping up the NHS, or providing bus services to the elderly in rural communities. And, for the many asylum-seeking men, women and children who have been displaced by warfare, exiled from their homes and compelled to start a new life in a strange place, fireworks are a massive, ear-walloping reminder of the horrors they thought they'd escaped.

So, if you're at a NYE party – and those around you are *ooh*ing and *aah*ing at the fireworks – don't feel bad if you shed a tear at the sheer sparkly waste of it all.

The Problem with New Year's Resolutions

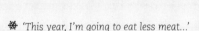
* 'This year, I'm going to eat less meat...'

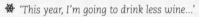
* 'This year, I'm going to drink less wine...'

* 'This year, I'm gonna try to be less of a prize-winning asshole...'

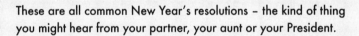
These are all common New Year's resolutions – the kind of thing you might hear from your partner, your aunt or your President.

They're all good, admirable ambitions, but the trouble is that even if your spouse, relative or leader of the free world commits to them for a while, there's a strong likelihood they won't stick to them for the long term. Precisely *because* they are New Year's resolutions.

There's a kind of strange,

unspoken understanding that making a New Year's resolution means you'll give something your 'best shot' – but, ultimately, you shouldn't be blamed if you can't persist with it.

This is where Snowflakes call BS.

As loud, proud, card-carrying Snowflakes, we wear our hearts on our sleeves. We are 100% *committed* to our beliefs – whether that's gender equality, halting the climate crisis or wearing vegan-friendly shoes. We don't have time for 'I'll try' or 'I'll give it a go'. We're like Yoda – (who takes 'green living' to a whole other level, by the way) – telling a churlish Luke Skywalker 'No! Try not! Do or do not. There is no try!'

On 31st December, you won't hear Greta T saying, 'This year, I'm going to try to be a bit less shouty' – and if you did, and you said to her, 'Good for you. This year, *I'm* going to try to wear more colours,' she'd probably stamp on your foot and poke you in the eye. She wouldn't enjoy it, but she'd do it all the same. And so would Yoda. (In fact, woe betide anyone who gets on the wrong side of Greta *or* Yoda... Catch them at the right moment and they can both be a lot of fun – especially at a house party or a music festival. But mess with them, and you've only got yourself to blame...)

Here are some examples of typical, vague, woolly, 'I'll give it my best shot', non-Snowflake New Year's resolutions...

This year, I will try to:

- read more books

- eat less sugary foods

- get more exercise

- stop smoking

Snowflakes don't make New Year's resolutions, but if we did (we don't), these are the kind of resolutions we would make...

This year, I will try to:

- write more tweets, calling out all the things that are wrong with society, and laying out my manifesto to try to fix them before it's too f***ing late.

- eat less meat and veg, reared and cultivated at the cost of our humanity and this planet's long-term viability.

- get more glue, so I can stick myself to more trains, trams, buses and planes.

- stop crying when I think about all the injustices in the world, and start my own online pressure group to enact change NOW!

If you identify as a non-Snowflake, and you find yourself at a New Year's Eve party, and you decide to tell someone who is on the Snowflake spectrum what you've chosen as your New Year's resolution, don't be surprised if they react strongly: by and large, they're unlikely to resort to actual violence, but they may well swear, vomit or sob uncontrollably at you.

Hearing other people's selfish, empty, under-delivering New Year's resolutions might just enrage, upset or depress you – which is a crummy way to start the new year and another good reason to stay at home on 31st December. As the old year makes way for the new, why not make a nice cup of caffeine-free herbal tea and settle down with a book. Perhaps this book – which you can resolve to share with all your like-minded friends and out-of-step relations.

The Problem with Conclusions

The problem with conclusions is that they spell the end – in this case, the end of this guide.

Whether you are a self-identifying Snowflake seeking festive help, or you've delved within these pages to better understand Snowflake culture and the struggles they face at Christmas, thank you for reading. We hope you have found aid or enlightenment, inspiration or understanding – ideally, all of these things.

Depending on how much you've enjoyed this book, now that it's finished, you can:

❄ **Treasure it.** Place it on a shelf, amongst other works you value, and come back to it each December, to remind yourself of its advice and suggestions.

❄ **Pass it on.** Gift it to a friend, family member, even a stranger on the bus – so that they too can benefit from its observations and ideas.

❄ **Recycle it.** The pages are printed on soft, absorbent, flushable paper. Knock yourself out.

In 1789, Benjamin Franklin wrote that nothing in the world can be certain 'except death and taxes'. But, if he were alive today, he might add '...and Christmas'.

Whatever your stance on geo and gender politics, sexuality or sustainability, Christmas is an inevitability.

Good luck with it.

Appendix A

A Snowflake's Christmas letter to Santa

Dear Santa Claus
(and your wife, and equally significant colleague, Mrs Claus),

I hope this finds you well and that you have been treating your workforce of vertically challenged elves with the dignity, rights and remuneration that they deserve.

Similarly, I trust that you have ceased your reckless genetic animal experimentation, that you have taken good care of Rudolph and his fellow reindeer, and that they have not been joined this year in the stables by 'Sebastian the Six-Legged Reindeer', 'Gordon the Glow-in-the-Dark Reindeer', or 'Jenny the Jet-Propelled Reindeer'.

This year, I have ~~strived striven strove~~ tried to be the best possible version of myself – a good, kind, compassionate, sensitive, non-judgemental, open-minded and principled human being. I am carbon-neutral, plant-based and lactose-free. If I have one vice, it might just be that I care too much – but there are worse failings... (I'm thinking of my Uncle Steve – the alcoholic, and pervert).

Based on all of this, I hope you will consider me deserving of gifts this Christmas. If so, these are things I would like:

1. An end to global warming (asap, please)

2. An end to the presidency of Donald Trump (again, asap please. BTW, while I do not condone violence, this can come about in whatever way you see fit – I'm happy to leave all options on the table...)

3. World peace (obvs)

4. HRH the Queen to take early retirement – and to appoint in her place not her son, Prince Charles (good, organic and sustainable farmer that he is – #deliciousbiscuits), but HRH (Her Righteous Highness) Greta Thunberg. I appreciate this may involve some paperwork, but it would be well worth the admin – to safeguard the planet and the lives of countless generations to come.

5. Snow this Christmas, please. Not so much that the elderly and the homeless freeze to death, but enough so that I can build a gender-neutral snowperson (I already have a name for it in mind – 'Mx Charlie') to take a selfie with.

6. No more Love Island, thanks. Where are the trans people? The overweight ones? Even the hairy ones? Also, no more Friends repeats, or old James Bond films. In fact, all television can just be nature documentaries moving forward... (But not too much Chris Packham, please.)

7. A weighted blanket – I read that they promote better sleep and reduce anxiety. I've got a LOT on my mind, so anything to help reduce stress would be a bonus.

8. One naughty treat: a sugar-free, nut-free, vegan chocolate yule log. YUM!

Thank you, Santa.

Love,
A. Snowflake

Appendix B

**Emotional Support Animals To Quell
Christmas-Induced Rage**

Picture credits

Page vi: Christmas tree: photograph by Ivonne Wierink/Shutterstock

Page x: Snowflake border: Aleksandrs Bondars/Shutterstock

Page 1: Snowflakes: photograph by Eugenio Marongiu/Shutterstock

Page 4: Greta Thunberg: photograph by Lëa-Kim Châteauneuf; Donald Trump: photograph by Gage Skidmore; Cows: photograph by Jenny Hill (via Unsplash)

Page 5: Mirror: photograph by Kirill (via Unsplash)

Page 8: Fir tree: photograph by gordontour

Page 9: Christmas tree: photograph by Jason Leung (via Unsplash); Dead tree: photograph by rame435/Shutterstock

Page 14: Family: photograph by DGLimages/Shutterstock; Plastic toys: photograph by Lifeman / Alamy Stock Photo

Page 18: Family: photograph by Roman Samborskyi/Shutterstock

Page 22: Carol singers, top: photograph by Digital Vision/Getty; Carol singers, bottom: photograph by DGLimages/iStock

Page 26-27: Death on the Pale Horse, Benjamin West, 1817

Page 32-33: Photograph by MR.Phakpoom Mahawat/Shutterstock

Page 42: Present-giving: photograph by Click and Photo/Shutterstock

Page 46: Christmas light: photograph by Ryan Moulton (via Upsplash); Christmas lights: photograph by can72/iStock

Page 56: illustrations by Meilun/Shutterstock

Page 63: turkey: illustration by Sudowoodo/Shutterstock

Page 66: photograph by Danie Nel Photography/Shutterstock

Page 68-69: Family meal: photograph by Roman Samborskyi/Shutterstock

Page 74: Party games: photograph by DGLimages/iStock

Page 82: Party image: photograph by Roman Samborskyi/Shutterstock

Page 83: Party image: photograph by gpointstudio/Shutterstock

Page 113: Remote control image: photograph by DGLimages/Shutterstock

Page 121: Protesters: photograph by Jacob Lund/Shutterstock

Page 125: Protesters: photograph by Halfpoint/Shutterstock

Page 131: Dog (left): photograph by Duffy Brook (via Unsplash); Dog (right): photograph by Charles Deluvio (via Unsplash); Guinea pigs: photograph by Bonnie Kittle (via Unsplash)

Page 132: Dog (top): photograph by Rhaúl V. Alva (via Unsplash); Dog (bottom): photograph by Jairo Alzate (via Unsplash); Cat: photograph by Ramiz Dedaković (via Unsplash)

Page 133: Monkey: photograph by Lewis Roberts (via Unsplash); Hedgehog: photograph by Keith Pittman (via Unsplash)